The Allies
of
Humanity

◆

BOOK ONE

The Allies

of

Humanity

◆

BOOK ONE

◆

AN URGENT MESSAGE
About the Extraterrestrial Presence
in the World Today

Marshall Vian Summers

AUTHOR OF

STEPS TO KNOWLEDGE: The Book of Inner Knowing

THE ALLIES OF HUMANITY BOOK ONE: An Urgent Message
About the Extraterrestrial Presence in the World Today

Edited by Darlene Mitchell

Book Design by Argent Associates, Boulder, CO

Cover art by Reed Novar Summers
> "To me, the cover image represents us on Earth with the black orb symbolizing
> the alien presence in the world today and the light behind it revealing this invis-
> ible presence to us which we would otherwise be unable to see. The star illumi-
> nating the Earth represents the Allies of Humanity giving us a new message and a
> new perspective on Earth's relationship to the Greater Community."

ISBN: 978-1-884238-45-1 THE ALLIES OF HUMANITY BOOK ONE: An Urgent
Message about the Extraterrestrial Presence in the World Today

Library of Congress Control Number: 2001 130786

This is the second edition of The Allies of Humanity Book One.

PUBLISHER'S CATALOGING-IN-PUBLICATION

Summers, Marshall.
    The allies of humanity book one : an urgent message about the
extraterrestrial presence in the world today / M.V. Summers
    p. cm.
    978-1-884238-45-1   001.942
                                               QB101-700606

The books of New Knowledge Library are published by The Society for The
Greater Community Way of Knowledge. The Society is a non-profit organization
dedicated to presenting The Greater Community Way of Knowledge.

To receive information about The Society's audio recordings, educational programs and contemplative services, please visit The Society on the worldwide web
or write:

THE SOCIETY FOR THE GREATER COMMUNITY WAY OF KNOWLEDGE
P.O. Box 1724 • Boulder, CO 80306-1724 • (303) 938-8401
society@greatercommunity.org
www.alliesofhumanity.org   www.newmessage.org

Dedicated to the great freedom movements

In the history of our world —

Both known and unknown.

CONTENTS

The four fundamental questions about the
extraterrestrial presence in the world today:

What is happening?

Why is it happening?

What does it mean?

How can we prepare?

It is uncommon enough to find a book that changes one's life, but far more extraordinary to encounter a work that has the potential to impact human history.

Nearly forty years ago, before there was an environmental movement, a courageous woman wrote a most provocative and controversial book that changed the course of history. Rachel Carson's *Silent Spring* spawned worldwide awareness of the dangers of environmental pollution and kindled an activist response which endures to this day. Among the first to publicly declare that the use of pesticides and chemical toxins was a threat to all life, Carson was ridiculed and vilified at first, even by many of her peers, but was ultimately considered one of the most important voices of the 20th century. *Silent Spring* is still widely regarded as the cornerstone of environmentalism.

Today, before there is prevalent public awareness of an ongoing extraterrestrial incursion in our midst, a similarly courageous man—a previously hidden spiritual teacher—comes forward bearing an extraordinary and disturbing communiqué from beyond our planetary sphere. With *The Allies of Humanity*, Marshall Vian Summers is the first spiritual leader of our time to unequivocally declare that the unbidden presence and clandestine actions of our extraterrestrial "visitors" constitute a profound threat to human freedom.

While at first, like Carson, Summers will surely meet with derision and disparagement, he may ultimately be recognized as one of the world's most important voices in the fields of extraterrestrial intelligence, human spirituality, and evolution of consciousness. Likewise, *The Allies of Humanity* may prove pivotal in ensuring the very future of our species—not only awakening us to the profound challenges of a silent alien invasion, but also igniting an unprecedented movement of resistance and empowerment.

Though the circumstances of the origin of this explosively controversial material may be problematic for some, the perspective it represents and the urgent message it conveys demand our deepest consideration and resolute response. Here we are all too plausibly confronted with the assertion that the increasing appearance of UFOs and other related phenomena are symptomatic of nothing less than a subtle and heretofore unopposed intervention by extraterrestrial forces who seek to exploit Earth's resources entirely for their own benefit.

How do we appropriately respond to such a disturbing and outrageous claim? Shall we ignore it or dismiss it out of hand, as many of Carson's detractors did? Or shall we investigate and attempt to understand exactly what is being offered here?

If we choose to investigate and understand, here is what we will find: A thorough review of recent decades of worldwide research into UFO activity and other apparently extraterrestrial phenomena (e.g., alien abduction and implants, animal mutilations, and even psychological "possession") yields ample evidence for the Allies' perspective; indeed, the information contained in the Allies' discourses stunningly clarifies issues that have puzzled researchers for years, accounting for much mysterious but persistent evidence.

Once we have investigated these matters and satisfied ourselves that the Allies' message is not only plausible but compelling, what then? Our considerations will inevitably lead to the inescapable conclusion that our predicament today has profound parallels to the incursion of European "civilization" into the Americas beginning in the 15th century, when indigenous peoples were unable to comprehend and adequately respond to the complexity and danger of the forces visiting their shores. The "visitors" came in the name of God, exhibiting impressive technology and purporting to offer a more advanced and more civilized way of life. (It is important to note that the European invaders were not "evil incarnate" but merely opportunistic, leaving in their wake a legacy of unintended devastation.)

Here is the point: The radical and wide-scale violation of fundamental freedoms that Native Americans subsequently experienced—including the rapid decimation of their population—is not only a monumental human tragedy, but also a powerful object lesson for our current situation. This time, we are all the native people of this one world, and unless we can collectively muster a more creative and unified response, we may suffer a similar fate. This is precisely the realization that *The Allies of Humanity* precipitates.

Yet, this is a book that can change lives, for it activates a deep inner calling that reminds us of our purpose in being alive at this moment in human history and brings us face to face with nothing less than our destiny. Here we are confronted with the most uncomfortable realization of all: The very future of humanity may well depend on how we respond to this message.

While *The Allies of Humanity* is profoundly cautionary, there is no inciting of fear or doom-and-gloom here. Instead, the message offers extraordinary hope in what is now a most dangerous and difficult situation. The obvious intention is to preserve and empower human freedom, and to catalyze personal and collective response to the alien intervention.

Fittingly, Rachel Carson herself once prophetically identified the very problem that impedes our ability to respond to this current crisis: "We still haven't become mature enough," she said, "to think of ourselves as only a very tiny part of a vast and incredible universe." Clearly, we have long needed a new understanding of ourselves, of our place in the cosmos, and of life in the Greater Community (the larger physical and spiritual universe into which we are now emerging). Fortunately, *The Allies of Humanity* serves as a gateway into a surprisingly substantial body of spiritual teachings and practices that promises to inculcate the requisite species maturity with a perspective that is neither earthbound nor anthropocentric, but instead is rooted in older, deeper and more universal traditions.

Ultimately, the message of *The Allies of Humanity* challenges nearly all of our fundamental notions of reality, simultaneously giving us our greatest opportunity for advancement and our greatest challenge for survival. While the current crisis threatens our self-determination as a species, it may also provide a much-needed foundation upon which to bring unity to the human race—a near impossibility without this larger context. With the perspective offered in *The Allies of Humanity* and the larger body of teachings represented by Summers, we are given both the imperative and the inspiration to join together in a deeper understanding to serve the further evolution of humanity.

◆

In his report for *Time Magazine*'s review of the 100 most influential voices of the 20th century, Peter Matthiessen wrote of Rachel Carson, "Before there was an environmental movement, there was one brave woman and her very brave book." Some years from now, we may be able to similarly say of Marshall Vian Summers: Before there was a human freedom movement to resist the extraterrestrial Intervention, there was one brave man and his very brave message, *The Allies of Humanity*. This time, may our response be more swift, more decisive, and more united.

—MICHAEL BROWNLEE
Journalist

NOTE TO READERS

The *Allies of Humanity* is being presented to prepare people for a whole new reality that is largely hidden and unrecognized in the world today. It provides a new perspective that empowers people to face the greatest challenge and opportunity that we, as a race, have ever encountered. The Allies Briefings contain a number of critical if not alarming statements about the growing extraterrestrial intervention and integration into the human race and about the extraterrestrial activities and hidden agenda. The purpose of the Allies Briefings is not to provide hard evidence about the reality of the ET visitation to our world, which is already well documented in many other fine books and research journals on the subject. The purpose of the Allies Briefings is to address the dramatic and far-reaching implications of this phenomenon, to challenge our human tendencies and assumptions regarding it and to alert the human family to the great threshold we now face. The Briefings provide a glimpse into the reality of intelligent life in the universe and what Contact will really mean. For many readers, what is revealed in *The Allies of Humanity* will be entirely new. For others, it will be a confirmation of things they have long felt and known.

Though this book provides an urgent message, it is also about moving towards a higher consciousness called "Knowledge," which includes a greater telepathic facility among people and between races. In light of this, the Allies Briefings were transmitted to the author from a multi-racial, extraterrestrial group of individuals who refer to themselves as the "Allies of Humanity." They describe themselves as physical beings from other worlds who have gathered in our solar system near the Earth for the purpose of observing the communications and activities of those alien races who are here in our world interfering in human affairs. They emphasize that they themselves are not physically present in our world and are providing needed wisdom, not technology or interference.

The Allies Briefings were given to the author over a one-year period. They offer perspective and vision into a complex subject which, despite decades of mounting evidence, continues to baffle researchers. Yet this perspective is not romantic, speculative or idealistic in its approach to this subject. To the contrary, it is bluntly realistic and uncompromising to the point where it may be quite challenging, even to a reader who is well versed in this subject.

Therefore, to receive what this book has to offer requires that you suspend, for a moment at least, many of the beliefs, assumptions and questions that you may have about extraterrestrial Contact and even about how this book was received. The contents of this book are like a message in a bottle sent here from beyond the world. Thus, we should not be so concerned about the bottle but about the message itself.

To truly understand this challenging message, we must confront and question many of the prevailing assumptions and tendencies

regarding the possibility and the reality of Contact. These include:
- denial;
- hopeful expectation;
- misinterpreting the evidence to affirm our beliefs;
- wanting and expecting salvation from the "visitors";
- believing that ET technology will save us;
- feeling hopeless and submissive to what we assume is a superior force;
- demanding government disclosure but not ET disclosure;
- condemning human leaders and institutions while maintaining unquestioned acceptance of the "visitors";
- assuming that because they have not attacked or invaded us, they must be here for our good;
- assuming that advanced technology equals advanced ethics and spirituality;
- believing that this phenomenon is a mystery when in fact it is a comprehensible event;
- believing that ETs in some way have claim to humanity and to this planet;
- and believing that humanity is irredeemable and cannot make it on its own.

The Allies Briefings challenge such assumptions and tendencies and explode many of the myths we currently have about who is visiting us and why they are here.

The Allies of Humanity Briefings give us a greater perspective and a deeper understanding of our destiny within a larger panorama of intelligent life in the universe. In order to achieve this, the Allies do not speak to our analytical mind but to Knowledge, the deeper part of our being where the truth, however clouded, can be directly discerned and experienced.

The Allies of Humanity Book One will raise many questions, which will require further exploration and contemplation. Its focus is not to provide names, dates and places but to provide a perspective on the ET presence in the world and on life in the universe that we as human beings could not otherwise have. While still living in isolation on the surface of our world, we cannot yet see and know what is happening regarding intelligent life beyond our borders. For this we need help, help of a very extraordinary kind. We may not recognize or accept such help at first. Yet it is here.

The Allies' stated purpose is to alert us to the risks of emerging into a Greater Community of intelligent life and to assist us in successfully crossing this great threshold in such a way that human freedom, sovereignty and self-determination can be preserved. The Allies are here to advise us of the need for humanity to establish our own "Rules of Engagement" during this unprecedented time. According to the Allies, if we are wise, prepared and united, we will then be able to take our destined place as a mature and free race in the Greater Community.

◆

Over the course of time that this series of briefings occurred, the Allies repeated certain key ideas that they felt were vital to our understanding. We have maintained these reiterations in the book in order to preserve the intention and integrity of their communication. Because of the urgent nature of the Allies' message and because of the forces in the world that would oppose this message, there is a wisdom and a necessity to these repetitions.

Following the publication of *The Allies of Humanity Book One* in 2001, the Allies provided a second set of Briefings to complete their vital message to humanity. *The Allies of Humanity Book Two*, published in 2005, presents startling new information on the interactions between races in our local universe and on the nature, purpose and most hidden activities of those races who are interfering in human affairs. Thanks to those readers who felt the urgency of the Allies' message and translated the Briefings into other languages, there is an expanding worldwide awareness of the reality of the Intervention.

We at New Knowledge Library consider that these two sets of Briefings contain what may be one of the most important messages being communicated in the world today. *The Allies of Humanity* is not just another book speculating about the UFO/ET phenomenon. It is a genuine transformational message aimed directly at the underlying purpose of the alien Intervention in order to raise the awareness that we will need to face the challenges and the opportunities that lie ahead.

—NEW KNOWLEDGE LIBRARY

WHO ARE THE ALLIES OF HUMANITY?

The Allies serve humanity because they serve the reclamation and expression of Knowledge everywhere in the Greater Community. They represent the wise in many worlds who support a greater purpose in life. Together they share a greater Knowledge and Wisdom that can be transferred across vast distances of space and across all the boundaries of race, culture, temperament and environment. Their wisdom is pervasive. Their skill is great. Their presence is hidden. They recognize you because they realize that you are an emerging race, emerging into a very difficult and competitive environment in the Greater Community.

◆

GREATER COMMUNITY SPIRITUALITY
Chapter 15: Who Serves Humanity?

. . . Over twenty years ago, a group of individuals from several different worlds gathered at a discreet location in our solar system near the Earth for the purpose of observing the alien visitation that is occurring in our world. From their hidden vantage point, they were able to determine the identity, organization and intentions of those visiting our world and monitor the visitors' activities.

This group of observers call themselves the "Allies of Humanity."

This is their report.

The
Briefings

◆

The Extraterrestrial Presence in the World Today

I t is a great honor for us to be able to present this information to all of you who are fortunate enough to hear this message. We are the Allies of Humanity. This transmission is being made possible by the presence of the Unseen Ones, the spiritual counselors who oversee the development of intelligent life both within your world and throughout the Greater Community of worlds.

We are not communicating through any mechanical device, but through a spiritual channel that is free from interference. Though we live in the physical, as do you, we are given the privilege to communicate in this way in order to deliver the information that we must share with you.

We represent a small group who are observing the events of your world. We come from the Greater Community. We do not interfere in human affairs. We have no establishment here. We have been sent for a very specific purpose—to witness the events that are occurring in your world and, given the opportunity to do so, to communicate to you what we see and what we know. For you live on the surface of your world and cannot see the affairs that surround it. Nor can you see clearly the visitation that is occurring in your world at this time or what it portends for your future.

We would like to give testimony to this. We are doing so at the request of the Unseen Ones, for we have been sent for this purpose. The information that we are about to impart to you may seem very challenging and startling. It is perhaps unexpected by many who will hear this message. We understand this difficulty, for we have had to face this within our own cultures.

As you hear the information, it may be difficult to accept at first, but it is vital for all who would seek to make a contribution in the world.

For many years we have been observing the affairs of your world. We seek no relations with humanity. We are not here on a diplomatic mission. We have been sent by the Unseen Ones to live in the proximity of your world in order to observe the events we are about to describe.

Our names are not important. They would be meaningless to you. And we shall not impart them for our own safety, for we must remain hidden in order that we may serve.

To begin, it is necessary for people everywhere to understand that humanity is emerging into a Greater Community of intelligent life. Your world is being "visited" by several alien races and by several different organizations of races. This has been actively going on for some time. There have been visitations throughout human history, but nothing of this magnitude. The advent of nuclear weapons and the destruction of your natural world have brought these forces to your shores.

There are many people in the world today, we understand, who are beginning to realize that this is occurring. And we understand as well that there are many interpretations of this visitation—what it could mean and what it could offer. And many of the people who are aware of these things are very hopeful and anticipate a great benefit for humanity. We understand. It is natural to expect this. It is natural to be hopeful.

The visitation in your world now is very extensive, so much so that people in all parts of the world are witnessing it and are experiencing its effects directly. What has brought these "visitors" from the Greater Community, these different organizations of beings, is not to promote the advancement of humanity or the spiritual education of humanity. What has brought these forces to your shores in such numbers with such intention are the resources of your world.

The visitation in your world now is very extensive, so much so that people in all parts of the world are witnessing it and are experiencing its effects directly.

This we understand may be difficult to accept at first because you cannot yet appreciate how beautiful your world is, how much it possesses and what a rare jewel it is in a Greater Community of barren worlds and empty space. Worlds such as yours are rare indeed. Most places in the Greater Community that are inhabited now have been colonized, and technology has made this possible. But worlds such as yours where life has evolved naturally, without the aid of technology, are far more rare than you might realize. Others take great notice of this, of course, for the biological resources of your world have been used by several races for millennia. It is considered a storehouse for some. And yet the development of human culture and dangerous weapons and the deterioration of these resources have caused the alien Intervention.

Perhaps you might wonder why diplomatic efforts are not established to contact the leaders of humanity. This is reasonable to ask, but the difficulty here is that there is no one to represent humanity, for your people are divided, and your nations oppose one another. It is also assumed by these visitors that we speak of that you are warlike and aggressive and that you would bring harm and hostility to the universe around you despite your good qualities.

Therefore, in our discourse we want to give you an idea of what is occurring, what it will mean for humanity and how it is related to your spiritual development, your social development and your future in the world and in the Greater Community of worlds itself.

People are unaware of the presence of alien forces, unaware of the presence of resource explorers, of those who would seek an alliance with humanity for their own benefit. Perhaps we should begin here by giving you an idea of what life is like beyond your shores, for you have not journeyed afar and cannot account for these things yourself.

You live in a part of the galaxy that is quite inhabited. Not all parts of the galaxy are so inhabited. There are great unexplored regions. There are many hidden races. Trade and commerce between worlds are only carried on in certain areas. The environment that you will emerge into is a very competitive one. The need for resources is experienced everywhere, and many technological societies have outstripped their world's natural resources and must trade, barter and travel to gain what they need. It is a very complicated situation. Many alliances are formed and conflicts do occur.

Perhaps at this point it is necessary to realize that the Greater

Community into which you are emerging is a difficult environment and a challenging one, and yet it brings great opportunity and great possibilities for humanity. However, for these possibilities and these advantages to be realized, humanity must prepare and come to learn what life in the universe is like. And it must come to understand what spirituality means within a Greater Community of intelligent life.

We understand from our own history that this is the greatest threshold that any world will ever face. It is not something, however, that you can plan for yourself. It is not something that you can design for your own future. For the very forces that would bring the Greater Community reality here are already present in the world. Circumstances have brought them here. They are here.

Perhaps this gives you an idea of what life is like beyond your borders. We do not want to create an idea that is fearful, but it is necessary for your own well-being and for your future that you have an honest appraisal and can come to see these things clearly.

The need to prepare for life in the Greater Community, we feel, is the greatest need there is in your world today. And yet, from our observation, people are preoccupied with their own affairs and their own problems in their daily lives, unaware of the greater forces that will change their destiny and affect their future.

The forces and groups who are here today represent several different alliances.

The forces and groups who are here today represent several different alliances. These different alliances are not united with each other in their efforts. Each alliance represents several different racial groups who are collaborating for the purpose of gaining access to your world's resources and maintaining this access. These different alliances are, in essence, competing with each other though they are not at war with one another. They see your world as a great prize, something they want to have for themselves.

This creates a very great challenge for your people, for the forces who are visiting you not only have advanced technology, but also strong social cohesion and are able to influence thought in the mental environment. You see, in the Greater Community, technology is easily acquired, and so the great advantage between competing societies is the ability to influence thought. This has taken on very sophisticated demonstrations. It represents a set of skills that humanity is only beginning to discover.

As a result, your visitors do not come armed with great weapons or with armies or with armadas of vessels. They come in relatively small groups, but they possess considerable skill in influencing people. This represents a more sophisticated and mature use of power in the Greater Community. It is this ability that humanity will have to cultivate in the future if it is to contend with other races successfully.

The visitors are here to gain humanity's allegiance. They do not want to destroy human establishments or the human presence. Instead, they wish to use these for their own benefit. Their intention is employment, not destruction. They feel that they are in the right because they believe that they are saving the world. Some even believe that they are saving humanity from itself. But this perspective does not serve your greater interests, nor does it foster wisdom or self-determination within the human family.

> The visitors are engaged in four fundamental activities in order to gain influence within your world.

Yet because there are forces of good within the Greater Community of Worlds, you have allies. We represent the voice of your allies, the Allies of Humanity. We are not here to use your resources or to take from you what you possess. We do not seek to establish humanity as a client state or as a colony for our own use. Instead, we wish to foster strength and wisdom within humanity because we support this throughout the Greater Community.

Our role, then, is quite essential, and our information is very needed because at this time even people who are aware of the presence of the visitors are not yet aware of their intentions. People do not understand the visitors' methods. And they do not comprehend the visitors' ethics or morality. People think the visitors are either angels or monsters. But in reality, they are very much like you in their needs. If you could see the world through their eyes, you would understand their consciousness and their motivation. But to do that, you would have to venture beyond your own.

The visitors are engaged in four fundamental activities in order to gain influence within your world. Each of these activities is unique, but they are all coordinated together. They are being carried out because humanity has been studied for a long time. Human thought, human behavior, human physiology and human religion have been studied for some time. These are well understood by your visitors and will be used for their own purposes.

The first area of activity of the visitors is to influence individuals in positions of power and authority. Because the visitors do not want to destroy anything in the world or harm the world's resources, they seek to gain influence over those whom they perceive to be in positions of power, within government and religion primarily. They seek contact, but only with certain individuals. They have the power to make this contact, and they have the power of persuasion. Not all whom they contact will be persuaded, but many will be. The promise of greater power, greater technology and world domination will intrigue and incite many individuals. And it is these individuals with whom the visitors will seek to establish a liaison.

There are very few people in the governments of the world who are being so affected, but their numbers are growing. The visitors understand the hierarchy of power because they themselves live by it, following their own chain of command, you might say. They are highly organized and very focused in their endeavors, and the idea of having cultures full of free-thinking individuals is largely foreign to them. They do not comprehend or understand individual freedom. They are like many technologically advanced societies in the Greater Community who function both within their respective worlds and in their establishments across vast reaches of space, utilizing a very well-established and rigid form of government and organization. They believe that humanity is chaotic and unruly, and they feel they are bringing order to a situation that they cannot themselves comprehend. Individual freedom is unknown to them, and they do not see its value. As a result, what they seek to establish in the world will not honor this freedom.

> The promise of greater power, greater technology and world domination will intrigue and incite many individuals. And it is these individuals with whom the visitors will seek to establish a liaison.

Therefore, their first area of endeavor is to establish a liaison with individuals in positions of power and influence in order to gain their allegiance and to persuade them of the beneficial aspects of relationship and shared purpose.

The second avenue of activity, which is perhaps the most difficult to consider from your perspective, is the manipulation of religious values and impulses. The visitors understand that humanity's greatest abilities also represent its greatest vulnerability. People's longing for individual redemption represents one of the greatest assets the human family has to offer, even to the Greater Community. But it is also your weakness. And it is these impulses and these values that will be used.

Several groups of the visitors wish to establish themselves as spiritual agents because they know how to speak in the mental environment. They can communicate to people directly, and unfortunately, because there are very few people in the world who can discern the difference between a spiritual voice and the visitors' voice, the situation becomes very difficult.

Therefore, the second area of activity is to gain people's allegiance through their religious and spiritual motivations. Actually, this can be done quite easily because humanity is not yet strong or developed in the mental environment. It is difficult for people to discern where these impulses are coming from. Many people want to give themselves to anything they think has a greater voice and a greater power. Your visitors can project images—images of your saints, of your teachers, of angels—images that are held dear and sacred within your world. They have cultivated this ability through many, many centuries of attempting to influence each other and by learning the ways of persuasion that are practiced in many places in the Greater Community. They consider you primitive, and so they feel they can exert this influence and use these methods upon you.

Here there is an attempt to contact those individuals who are considered sensitive, receptive and naturally given to be coopera-tive. Many people will be selected, but a few will be chosen based upon these particular qualities. Your visitors will seek to gain al-legiance with these individuals, to gain their trust and to gain their devotion, telling the recipients that the visitors are here to uplift hu-manity spiritually, to give humanity new hope, new blessings and new power—indeed promising the things that people want so dearly but have not yet found themselves. Perhaps you may wonder, "How can such a thing occur?" But we can assure you that it is not difficult once you learn these skills and abilities.

The effort here is to pacify and to reeducate people through spiritual persuasion. This "Pacification Program" is used differently with different religious groups depending upon their ideals and their temperament. It is always aimed at receptive individuals. Here it is hoped that people will lose their sense of discernment and will become wholly trusting of the greater power that they feel is being given to them by the visitors. Once this allegiance is established, it becomes increasingly difficult for people to discern what they know within themselves from what is being told to them. It is a very subtle but very pervasive form of persuasion and manipulation. We shall speak more on this as we proceed.

Let us now mention the third area of activity, which is to estab-lish the visitors' presence in the world and to have people become used to this presence. They want humanity to become acclimated to this very great change that is occurring in your midst—to have you become acclimated to the visitors' physical presence and to their effect on your own mental environment. To serve this purpose, they will create establishments here, though not in view. These establishments will be hidden, but they will be very powerful in casting an influence on human populations that are near them. The visitors will take great care and time to make sure that these establishments are effective and that enough people are in allegiance to them. It is these people who will guard and preserve the visitors' presence.

This is exactly what is occurring in your world at this time. It represents a great challenge and unfortunately a great risk. This very same thing that we are describing has happened so many times in so many places in the Greater Community. And emerging races such as your own are always the most vulnerable. Some emerging races are able to establish their own awareness, ability and cooperation to the extent that they can offset outside influences such as these and establish a presence and a position in the Greater Community. Yet many races, before they even attain this freedom, fall under the control and influence of foreign powers.

We understand that this information may incite considerable fear and perhaps denial or confusion. But as we observe events, we realize that there are very few people who are aware of the situation as it actually exists. Even those people who are becoming aware of the presence of alien forces are not in a position and do not have the vantage point from which they can see the situation clearly. And being ever hopeful and optimistic, they seek to give this great phenomenon as much positive meaning as they can.

> Those who engage in space travel do not necessarily represent the spiritually advanced . . .

However, the Greater Community is a competitive environment, a difficult environment. Those who engage in space travel do not necessarily represent the spiritually advanced, for those who are spiritually advanced seek insulation from the Greater Community. They do not seek commerce. They do not seek to influence other races or to engage in the very complex array of relationships that are established for mutual trade and benefit. Instead, the spiritually advanced seek to remain hidden. This is a very different understanding, perhaps, but a necessary one for you to come to comprehend the great predicament that humanity is facing. Yet this predicament holds great possibilities. We would like to speak about these now.

> People everywhere have great spiritual gifts that can enable them to see and to know clearly. These gifts are needed now.

Despite the gravity of the situation that we are describing, we do not feel that these circumstances are a tragedy for humanity. Indeed, if these circumstances can be recognized and understood, and if the preparation for the Greater Community, which now exists in the world, can be utilized, studied and applied, then people everywhere of good conscience will have the ability to learn Greater Community Knowledge and Wisdom.

Thus, people everywhere will be able to find the basis for cooperation so that the human family can finally establish a unity that has never been established here before. For it will take the overshadowing of the Greater Community to unite humanity. And this overshadowing is occurring now.

It is your evolution to emerge into a Greater Community of intelligent life. It will happen whether you are prepared or not. It must occur. Preparation, then, becomes the key. Understanding and clarity—these are the things that are necessary and needed in your world at this time.

People everywhere have great spiritual gifts that can enable them to see and to know clearly. These gifts are needed now. They need to be recognized, employed and shared freely. It is not merely up to a great teacher or a great saint in your world to do this. It must be cultivated by many more people now. For the situation brings with it necessity, and if necessity can be embraced, it brings with it great opportunity.

However, the requirements to learn about the Greater Community and to begin to experience Greater Community Spirituality are tremendous. Never before have human beings had to learn such things in such a short period of time. Indeed, such things have rarely been learned ever by anyone in your world before. But now the need has changed. The circumstances are different. Now there are new influences in your midst, influences that you can feel and that you can know.

The visitors seek to disable people from having this vision and this Knowledge within themselves, for your visitors do not have it within themselves. They do not see its value. They do not understand its reality. In this, humanity as a whole is more advanced than they are. But this is only a potential, a potential which must now be cultivated.

The alien presence in the world is growing. It is growing every day, every year. Many more people are falling under its persuasion, losing their ability to know, becoming confused and distracted, believing in things that can only weaken them and make them impotent in the face of those who would seek to use them for their own purposes.

Humanity is an emerging race. It is vulnerable. It is facing a set of circumstances and influences now which it has never had to face before. You have only evolved to compete with each other. You have never had to compete with other forms of intelligent life. Yet it is this competition that will strengthen you and will call forth your greatest attributes if the situation can be clearly seen and understood.

It is the role of the Unseen Ones to foster this strength. The Unseen Ones, whom you would rightly call angels, do not only speak to the human heart but to hearts everywhere who are able to listen and who have gained the freedom to listen.

We come, then, with a difficult message, but a message of promise and hope. Perhaps it is not the message that people want to hear. It is certainly not the message that the visitors would promote. It is a message that can be shared from person to person, and it will be shared because it is natural to do so. Yet the visitors and those who have come under their persuasion will oppose such an awareness. They do not want to see an independent humanity. That is not their purpose. They do not even believe it is beneficial. Therefore, it is our sincere desire that these ideas be considered without trepidation, but with a serious mind and a deep concern that are well justified here.

There are many people in the world today, we understand, who feel that a great change is coming for humanity. The Unseen Ones have told us these things. Many causes are attributed to this sense of change. And many outcomes are predicted. Yet unless you can begin to comprehend the reality that humanity is emerging into a Greater Community of intelligent life, you do not yet have the right context for understanding the destiny of humanity or the great change that is occurring in the world.

From our perspective, people are born into their time to serve that time. This is a teaching in Greater Community Spirituality, a teaching of which we are students as well. It teaches freedom and the power of shared purpose. It grants authority to the individual and to the individual who can join with others—ideas which are rarely accepted or adopted in the Greater Community, for the Greater Community is not the heavenly state. It is a physical reality with the rigors of survival and all that that entails. All beings within this reality must contend with these needs and issues. And in this, your visitors are more like you than you realize. They are not incomprehensible. They would seek to be incomprehensible, but they can be understood. You have the power to do this, but you must see with clear eyes. You must see with a greater vision and know with a greater intelligence, which you have the possibility to cultivate within yourselves.

It is necessary for us now to speak more regarding the second area of influence and persuasion because this has great importance, and it is our sincere desire that you will understand these things and consider them for yourself.

The religions of the world hold the key to human dedication and human allegiance, more than governments, more than any other institution. This speaks well for humanity because religions such as these are often hard to find in the Greater Community. Your world is rich in this respect, but your strength is also where you are weak and vulnerable. Many people want to be divinely guided and appointed, to give over the reins of their own lives and to have a greater spiritual power direct them, counsel them and preserve them. This is a genuine desire, but within a Greater Community context, considerable wisdom must be cultivated in order for this desire to be fulfilled. It is very sad for us to see how people will give their authority away so easily—something they have never even fully had, they will give away willingly to those who are unknown to them.

This message is destined to reach people who have a greater spiritual affinity. Therefore, it is necessary that we elaborate on this subject. We advocate a spirituality that is taught in the Greater Community, not the spirituality that is governed by nations, governments or political alliances, but a natural spirituality—the ability to know, to see and to act. And yet this is not emphasized by your visitors. They seek to have people believe that the visitors are their family, that the visitors are their home, that the visitors are their brothers and sisters, their mothers and fathers. Many people want to believe, and so they believe. People want to give over their personal authority, and so it is given over. People want to see friends and salvation in the visitors, and so this is what they are shown.

> People want to see friends and salvation in the visitors, and so this is what they are shown.

It will take great sobriety and objectivity in order to see through these deceptions and these difficulties. It will be necessary for people to do this if humanity is to successfully emerge into the Greater Community and maintain its freedom and its self-determination in an environment of greater influences and greater forces. In this, your world could be overtaken without firing a shot, for violence is considered primitive and crude and is rarely employed in matters such as this.

Perhaps you may ask, "Does this mean that there is an invasion of our world?" We must say that the answer to this is "yes," an invasion of the most subtle kind. If you can entertain these thoughts and consider them seriously, you will be able to see these things for yourself. The evidence of this invasion is everywhere. You can see how human ability is offset by the desire for happiness, peace and security, how people's vision and ability to know are hampered by influences even within their own cultures. How much greater these influences will be within a Greater Community environment.

This is the difficult message that we must present. This is the message that must be said, the truth that must be spoken, the truth that is vital and cannot wait. It is so necessary for people now to learn a greater Knowledge, a greater Wisdom and a greater Spirituality so that they may find their true abilities and be able to use them effectively.

Your freedom is at stake. The future of your world is at stake. It is because of this that we have been sent here to speak for the Allies of Humanity. There are those in the universe who are keeping Knowledge and Wisdom alive and who practice a Greater Community Spirituality. They do not travel all about, casting influence over different worlds. They do not take people against their will. They do not steal your animals and your plants. They do not cast influence over your governments. They do not seek to breed with humanity in order to create a new leadership here. Your allies do not interfere in human affairs. They do not manipulate human destiny. They watch from afar and they send emissaries such as ourselves, at great risk to us, to give counsel and encouragement and to clarify things when that becomes necessary. We, therefore, come in peace with a vital message.

Now we must speak of the fourth area in which your visitors seek to establish themselves, and that is through interbreeding. They cannot live in your environment. They need your physical stamina. They need your natural affinity with the world. They need your reproductive abilities. They also want to bond with you because they understand that this creates allegiance. This, in a way, establishes their presence here because the offspring of such a program will have blood relations in the world and yet will have allegiance to the visitors. Perhaps this seems incredible, yet it is so very real.

The visitors are not here to take your reproductive abilities away from you. They are here to establish themselves. They want humanity to believe in them and to serve them. They want humanity to work for them. They will promise anything, offer anything and do anything to achieve this goal. Yet though their persuasion is great, their numbers are small. But their influence is growing and their program of interbreeding, which has been underway for several generations, will eventually be effective. There will be human beings of greater intelligence but who do not represent the human family. Such things are possible and have occurred countless times in the Greater Community. You have only to look at your own history to see the impact of cultures and races upon one another and to see how dominating and how influential these interactions can be.

Thus, we bring with us important news, serious news. But you must take heart, for this is not a time for ambivalence. This is not a time to seek escape. This is not a time to concern yourself with your own happiness. This is a time to contribute to the world, to strengthen the human family and to call forth those natural abilities that exist in people—the ability to see, to know and to act in harmony with one another. These abilities can offset the influence that is being cast upon humanity at this time, but these abilities must grow and be shared. It is of the utmost importance.

This is our counsel. It comes with good intentions. Be glad that you have allies in the Greater Community, for allies you will need.

You are entering a greater universe, filled with forces and influences that you have not yet learned how to counteract. You are entering a greater panorama of life. And you must prepare for this. Our words are but part of the preparation. A preparation is being sent into the world now. It does not come from us. It comes from the Creator of all life. It comes at just the right time. For this is the time for humanity to become strong and wise. You have the ability to do this. And the events and circumstances of your life create a great need for this.

This is not a time to seek escape. This is not a time to concern yourself with your own happiness. This is a time to contribute to the world, to strengthen the human family . . .

The Challenge to Human Freedom

Humanity is approaching a very dangerous and very important time in its collective development. You are on the verge of emerging into a Greater Community of intelligent life. You will be encountering other races of beings who are coming to your world seeking to protect their interests and to discover what opportunities may lie ahead. They are not angels or angelic beings. They are not spiritual entities. They are beings who are coming to your world for resources, for alliances and to gain an advantage in an emerging world. They are not evil. They are not holy. In that, they are also much like you. They are simply driven by their needs, their associations, their beliefs and their collective goals.

This is a very great time for humanity, but humanity is not prepared. From our vantage point, we can see this on a larger scale. We do not involve ourselves with the daily lives of individuals in the world. We do not attempt to persuade governments or to lay claim to certain parts of the world or to certain resources that exist here. Instead, we observe, and we wish to report what we observe, for this is our mission in being here.

The Unseen Ones have told us that there are many people today who feel a strange discomfort, a sense of vague urgency, a feeling that something is going to happen and that something must be done. Perhaps there is nothing within their daily sphere of experience that justifies these deeper feelings, that verifies the importance of these feelings, or that gives substance to their expression. We can understand this because we have been through similar things ourselves in our own histories. We represent several races joined together in our small alliance to support the emergence of Knowledge and Wisdom in the universe, particularly with races that are on the threshold of emerging into the Greater Community. These emerging races are particularly vulnerable to foreign influence and manipulation. They are particularly vulnerable to misunderstanding their situation and understandably so, for how could they comprehend the meaning and the complexity of life within the Greater Community? That is why we wish to play our small part in preparing and in educating humanity.

> . . .there are many people today who feel a strange discomfort, a sense of vague urgency, a feeling that something is going to happen and that something must be done.

In our first discourse, we gave a broad description of the visitors' involvement in four areas. The first area is the influence on important people in positions of power in governments and at the head of religious institutions. The second area of influence is on people who have a spiritual inclination and who wish to open themselves to the greater powers that exist in the universe. The third area of involvement is the visitors' building of establishments in the world in strategic locations, near population centers, where their influence on the mental environment can be exercised. And lastly, we spoke of their program of interbreeding with humanity, a program which has been underway for quite some time.

We understand how troubling this news may be and perhaps how disappointing it may be to many people who had high hopes and expectations that visitors from beyond would bring blessings and great benefit to humanity. It is natural perhaps to assume and to expect these things, but the Greater Community into which humanity is emerging is a difficult and competitive environment, particularly in areas in the universe where many different races compete with each other and interact for trade and commerce. Your world exists in such an area. This may seem incredible to you because it has always seemed that you lived in isolation, alone within the vast emptiness of space. But really you live in an inhabited part of the universe where trade and commerce have been established and where traditions, interactions and associations are all longstanding. And to your benefit, you live in a beautiful world—a world of great biological diversity, a splendid place in contrast to the starkness of so many other worlds.

However, this also gives your situation great urgency and poses a genuine risk, for you possess what many others want for themselves. They do not seek to destroy you but to gain your allegiance and your alliance so that your existence in the world and your activities here can be for their benefit. You are emerging into a mature and complicated set of circumstances. Here you cannot be like little children and believe and hope for the blessings of all whom you may

We represent several races joined together in our small alliance to support the emergence of Knowledge and Wisdom in the universe . . .

encounter. You must become wise and discerning, as we, through our difficult histories, have had to become wise and discerning. Now humanity will have to learn about the ways of the Greater Community, about the intricacies of interaction between races, about the complexities of trade and about the subtle manipulations of associations and alliances that are established between worlds. It is a difficult but important time for humanity, a time of great promise if true preparation can be undertaken.

You are emerging into a mature and complicated set of circumstances. Here you cannot be like little children and believe and hope for the blessings of all whom you may encounter.

In this, our second discourse, we would like to speak in greater detail about the intervention into human affairs by various groups of visitors, what this may mean for you and what this will require. We come not to incite fear but to provoke a sense of responsibility, to engender a greater awareness and to encourage preparation for the life that you are entering into, a greater life but a life with greater problems and challenges as well.

We have been sent here through the spiritual power and presence of the Unseen Ones. Perhaps you will think of them in a friendly way as angels, but in the Greater Community their role is greater and their involvement and their alliances are deep and penetrating. Their spiritual power is here to bless sentient beings in all worlds and in all places and to promote the development of the deeper Knowledge and Wisdom that will make possible the peaceful emergence of relations, both between worlds and within worlds. We are here on their behalf. They have asked us to come. And they have given us much of the information that we have, infor-

We come not to incite fear but to provoke a sense of responsibility . . .

mation that we could not collect ourselves. From them we have learned a great deal about your nature. We have learned a great deal about your abilities, your strengths, your weaknesses and your great vulnerability. We can comprehend these things because the worlds that we have come from have passed through this great threshold of emergence into the Greater Community. We have learned a great deal, and we have suffered much from our own mistakes, mistakes that we hope humanity will avoid.

We come then not only with our own experience, but with a deeper awareness and a deeper sense of purpose that has been given to us by the Unseen Ones. We observe your world from a location nearby, and we monitor the communications of those who are visiting you. We know who they are. We know where they come from and why they are here. We do not compete with them, for we are not here to exploit the world. We consider ourselves to be the Allies of Humanity, and we hope in time that you will consider us to be such, for such we are. And though we cannot prove this, we hope to demonstrate this through our words and through the wisdom of our counsel. We hope to prepare you for what lies ahead. We come in our mission with a sense of urgency, for humanity is way behind in its preparation for the Greater Community. Many earlier attempts decades ago to make contact with human beings and to prepare human beings for their future proved to be unsuccessful. Only a few people could be reached, and as we have been told, many of these contacts were misconstrued and were used by others for different purposes.

Therefore, we have been sent in the place of those who came

> We come in our mission with a sense of urgency, for humanity is way behind in its preparation for the Greater Community.

before us to offer help to humanity. We work together in our united cause. We do not represent a great military power but more a secret and holy alliance. We do not want to see the kind of affairs that exist in the Greater Community perpetrated here within your world. We do not want to see humanity become a client state of a greater network of powers. We do not want to see humanity lose its freedom and its self-determination. These are real risks. Because of this, we encourage you to consider our words deeply, without fear, if that is possible, and with the kind of conviction and determination that we know resides in all human hearts.

We do not want to see humanity become a client state of a greater network of powers.

Today and tomorrow and the day after, great activity is underway and will be underway to establish a network of influence over the human race by those who are visiting the world for their own purposes. They feel that they are coming here to save the world from humanity. Some even believe they are here to save humanity from itself. They feel that they are in the right and do not consider that their actions are inappropriate or unethical. According to their ethics, they are doing what is considered to be reasonable and important. However, for all freedom-loving beings, such an approach cannot be justified.

We observe the visitors' activities, which are growing. Every year, there are more of them here. They are coming from afar. They are bringing supplies. They are deepening their engagement and involvement. They are establishing stations of communication in many places in your solar system. They are observing all of your initial forays into space, and they will counter and destroy anything that they feel will interfere with their activities. They are seeking to establish control not only of your world but of the area around your world. This is because there are competing forces here. Each represents the alliance of several races.

Now let us address the last of the four areas that we spoke of in our first discourse. This has to do with the visitors interbreeding with the human species. Let us give you a bit of history first. Many thousands of years ago, in your time, several races came to interbreed with humanity to give humanity a greater intelligence and adaptability. This led to the rather sudden emergence of what we understand is called "Modern Man." This has given you dominance and power in your world. This occurred long ago.

However, the interbreeding program that is occurring now is not the same at all. It is being undertaken by a different set of beings and by different alliances. Through interbreeding, they are seeking to establish a human being who will be part of their association yet who can survive within your world and who can have a natural affinity with the world. Your visitors cannot live on the surface of your world. They must either seek shelter underground, which they are doing, or they must live aboard their own craft, which they often keep hidden in large bodies of water. They want to interbreed with humanity to protect their interests here, which are primarily the resources of your world. They want to have human allegiance assured, and so for several generations they have been involved in an interbreeding program, which within the last twenty years has become quite extensive.

They are observing all of your initial forays into space, and they will counter and destroy anything that they feel will interfere with their activities.

Their purpose is twofold. First, as we have mentioned, the visitors want to create a human-like being who can live within your world but who will be bonded to them and who will have a greater set of sensitivities and abilities. The second purpose of this program is to influence all those that they encounter and to encourage people to assist them in their undertaking. The visitors want and need human assistance. This furthers their program in all respects. They consider you valuable. However, they do not consider you to be their peers or their equals. Useful, that is how you are perceived. So, in all whom they will encounter, in all whom they will take, the visitors will seek to engender this sense of their superiority, their value and the worth and the significance of their endeavors in the world. The visitors will tell all whom they contact that they are here for the good, and they will assure those that they have captured that they need not fear. And with those who seem particularly receptive, they will attempt to establish alliances—a shared sense of purpose, even a shared sense of identity and family, of heritage and destiny.

In their program, the visitors have studied human physiology and psychology very extensively, and they will take advantage of what people want, particularly those things that people want but have not been able to gain for themselves, such as peace and order, beauty and tranquility. These will be offered and some people will believe. Others will simply be used as is needed.

Here it is necessary to understand that the visitors believe that this is entirely appropriate in order to preserve the world. They feel that they are doing humanity a great service, and so they are wholehearted in their persuasions. Unfortunately, this demonstrates a great truth about the Greater Community—that true Wisdom and true Knowledge are as rare in the universe as they must seem within your world. It is natural for you to hope and to expect that other races have outgrown deviousness, selfish pursuits, competition and conflict. But, alas, this is not the case. Greater technology does not raise the mental and spiritual strength of individuals.

Today there are many people who are being taken against their will repeatedly. Because humanity is very superstitious and seeks to deny things that it cannot understand, this unfortunate activity is being carried on with considerable success. Even now, there are hybrid individuals, part-human, part-alien, walking in your world. There are not many of them, but their numbers will grow in the future. Perhaps you will meet one some day. They will look the same as you but be different. You will think they are human beings, but something essential will seem to be missing in them, something that is valued within your world. It is possible to be able to discern and to identify these individuals, but in order to do so, you would have to become skilled in the mental environment and learn what Knowledge and Wisdom mean in the Greater Community.

> It is natural for you to hope and to expect that other races have outgrown deviousness, selfish pursuits, competition and conflict. But, alas, this is not the case. Greater technology does not raise the mental and spiritual strength of individuals.

We feel that learning this is of the utmost importance, for we see all that is happening in your world from our vantage point, and the Unseen Ones counsel us regarding things we cannot see or have access to. We understand these events, for they have happened countless times in the Greater Community, as influence and persuasion are cast upon races that are either too weak or too vulnerable to respond effectively.

We hope and we trust that none of you who may hear this message will think that these intrusions into human life are beneficial. Those who are being affected will be influenced to think that these encounters are beneficial, both for themselves and for the world. People's spiritual aspirations, their desire for peace and harmony, family and inclusion will all be addressed by the visitors. These things that represent something so special about the human family are, without wisdom and preparation, a sign of your great vulnerability. Only those individuals who are strong with Knowledge and Wisdom could see the deception behind these persuasions. Only they are in a position to see the deception that is being perpetrated upon the human family. Only they can protect their minds against the influence that is being cast in the mental environment in so many places in the world today. Only they will see and know.

... we encourage you not to believe that the taking of human beings and their children and their families has any benefit for humanity at all. We must emphasize this.

Our words will not be enough. Men and women must learn to see and to know. We can only encourage this. Our coming here to your world has occurred in accordance with the presentation of the teaching in Greater Community Spirituality, for the preparation is here now and that is why we can be a source of encouragement. If the preparation were not here, we would know that our admonitions and our encouragement would not be adequate and would not be successful. The Creator and the Unseen Ones want to prepare humanity for the Greater Community. In fact, this is the most important need of humanity at this time.

Therefore, we encourage you not to believe that the taking of human beings and their children and their families has any benefit for humanity at all. We must emphasize this. Your freedom is precious. Your individual freedom and your freedom as a race are precious. It has taken us so long to regain our freedom. We do not want to see you lose yours.

The interbreeding program that is occurring in the world will continue. The only way that it can be stopped is by people gaining this greater awareness and sense of inner authority. Only this will bring these intrusions to an end. Only this will uncover the deception behind them. It is hard for us to imagine how awful this must be for your people, for those men and women, for those little ones, who are undergoing this treatment, this re-education, this pacification. To our values, this seems abhorrent, and yet we know that these things occur in the Greater Community and have occurred since before memory.

Perhaps our words will generate more and more questions. This is healthy and this is natural, but we cannot answer all of your questions. You must find the means to gain the answers for yourselves. But you cannot do this without a preparation, and you cannot do this without an orientation. At this time, humanity as a whole, we understand, cannot differentiate between a Greater Community demonstration and a spiritual manifestation. This is truly a difficult situation because your visitors can project images, they can speak to people through the mental environment and their voices can be received and expressed through people. They can cast this kind of influence because humanity does not yet have this kind of skill or discernment.

Humanity is not united. It is broken apart. It is in contention

Humanity is not united. It is broken apart. It is in contention with itself. This makes you extremely vulnerable to outside interference and manipulation.

with itself. This makes you extremely vulnerable to outside interference and manipulation. It is understood by your visitors that your spiritual desires and inclinations make you particularly vulnerable and particularly good subjects for their use. How difficult it is to gain true objectivity regarding these things. Even where we have come from, it has been a great challenge. But for those who wish to remain free and to exercise self-determination in the Greater Community, they must develop these skills, and they must preserve their own resources in order to avoid being required to seek them from others. If your world loses its self-sufficiency, it will lose much of its freedom. If you must go beyond your world to seek the resources you need to live, then you will lose much of your power to others. Because the resources of your world are rapidly diminishing, this is a grave concern for those of us who watch from afar. It is also of concern to your visitors, for they want to prevent the destruction of your environment, not for you but for them.

The interbreeding program has only one purpose, and that is to enable the visitors to establish a presence and a commanding influence within the world. Do not think that the visitors are lacking something that they need from you other than your resources. Do not think that they need your humanity. They only want your humanity to assure themselves of their position in the world. Do not be flattered. Do not indulge yourself in such thoughts. They are unwarranted. If you can learn to see the situation clearly as it really is, you will see and you will know these things for yourself. You will understand why we are here and why humanity needs allies in a Greater Community of intelligent life. And you will see the importance of learning greater Knowledge and Wisdom and of learning

Greater Community Spirituality.

Because you are emerging into an environment where these things become vital for success, for freedom, for happiness and for strength, you will need greater Knowledge and Wisdom in order to establish yourselves as an independent race in the Greater Community. However, your independence is being lost with each passing day. And you may not see the loss of your freedom, though perhaps you may feel it in some way. How could you see it? You cannot go outside your world and witness the events that surround it. You do not have access to the political and commercial involvements of the alien forces operating in the world today to understand their complexity, their ethics or their values.

Never think that any race in the universe that travels for commerce is spiritually advanced. Those who seek commerce seek advantage. Those who travel from world to world, those who are resource explorers, those who seek to plant their own flags are not what you would consider to be spiritually advanced. We do not consider them to be spiritually advanced. There is worldly power, and there is spiritual power. You can understand the difference between these things, and now it is necessary to see this difference within a larger environment.

We come, then, with a sense of commitment and strong encouragement for you to maintain your freedom, to become strong and discerning and not to give into persuasions or promises of peace, power and inclusion from those you do not know. And do not let yourself be comforted into thinking that all will turn out well for humanity or even for you personally, for this is not wisdom. For the wise in any place must learn to see the reality of life around them and learn to negotiate this life in a beneficial way.

Therefore, receive our encouragement. We shall speak again concerning these matters and illustrate the importance of gaining discernment and discretion. And we shall speak more about the involvement of your visitors in the world in areas that are very important for you to understand. We hope that you can receive our words.

A Great Warning

We have been anxious to speak more with you regarding the affairs of your world and to help you come to see, if possible, what we are seeing from our vantage point. We realize this is difficult to receive and will cause considerable anxiety and concern, but you must be informed.

The situation is very grave from our perspective, and we think it would be a tremendous misfortune if people were not informed correctly. There is so much deception in the world that you live in, and in many other worlds as well, that the truth, though apparent and obvious, goes unrecognized, and its signs and messages go undetected. We, therefore, hope that our presence can help clarify the picture and help you and others to see what is truly there. We do not have these compromises in our perception, for we were sent to witness the very things that we are describing.

Over time, perhaps you would be able to know these things on your own, but you do not have this kind of time. The time now is short. Humanity's preparation for the appearance of forces from the Greater Community is far behind schedule. Many important people have not responded. And the intrusion into the world has accelerated at a far greater pace than was originally thought to be possible.

We come with little time to spare, and yet we come with encouragement for you to share this information. As we have indicated in our previous messages, the world is being infiltrated and the mental environment is being conditioned and prepared. The intention is not to eradicate human beings but to employ them, to have them become workers for a greater "collective." The institutions of the world and most certainly the natural environment are valued, and it is the preference of the visitors that these be preserved for their use. They cannot live here, and so to gain your allegiance, they are employing many of the techniques that we have described. We will continue in our description to clarify these things.

Our arrival here has been thwarted by several factors, not the least of which is a lack of readiness of those whom we must reach directly. Our speaker, the author of this book, is the only one with whom we have been able to establish a firm contact, so we must give our speaker the fundamental information.

From the perspective of your visitors, as we have learned, the United States is considered the world leader, and so the greatest amount of emphasis will be placed here. But other major nations as well will be contacted, for they are recognized to hold power, and power is understood by the visitors, for they follow the dictates of power without question and to a much greater degree than is even apparent in your world.

Attempts will be made to persuade the leaders of the strongest nations to become receptive to the presence of the visitors and to receive gifts and inducements for cooperation with the promise of mutual benefit, and even the promise of world dominion to some. There will be those in the corridors of power in the world who will respond to these inducements, for they will think that there is a great opportunity here to take humanity beyond the specter of nuclear war into a new community upon the earth, a community which they will lead for their own purposes. Yet these leaders are deceived, for they will not be given the keys to this realm. They will simply be the arbiters in the transition of power.

This you must understand. It is not so complex. From our perspective and vantage point, it is obvious. We have seen this occur elsewhere. It is one of the ways that established organizations of races who have their own collectives recruit emerging worlds such as yours. They believe firmly that their agenda is virtuous and for the betterment of your world, for humanity is not highly respected, and though you are virtuous in certain ways, your liabilities far outweigh your potential, from their perspective. We do not hold this view or we would not be in the position that we are in, and we would not be offering our services to you as the Allies of Humanity.

Therefore, there is a great difficulty now in discernment, a great challenge. The challenge is for humanity to understand who its allies really are and to be able to distinguish them from its potential adversaries. There are no neutral parties in this matter. The world is far too valuable, its resources recognized as being unique and of considerable worth. There are no neutral parties who are involved in human affairs. The true nature of the alien Intervention is to exert influence and control and eventually to establish dominion here.

We are not the visitors. We are observers. We claim no rights to your world, and we have no agenda to establish ourselves here. For this reason, our names are hidden, for we do not pursue relations with you beyond our ability to provide our counsel in this way. We cannot control the outcome. We can only advise you as to the choices and decisions that your people must make in light of these greater events.

The challenge is for humanity to understand who its allies really are and to be able to distinguish them from its potential adversaries. There are no neutral parties in this matter.

Humanity has great promise and has cultivated a rich spiritual heritage, but it is without education regarding the Greater Community into which it is emerging. Humanity is divided and contentious within itself, thus making it vulnerable to manipulation and to intrusion from beyond your borders. Your peoples are preoccupied with the concerns of the day, but the reality of tomorrow is not recognized. What profit could you possibly gain by ignoring the greater movement of the world and by assuming that the Intervention that is occurring today is for your benefit? Surely there is not one amongst you who could say this if you but saw the reality of the situation.

In a way, it is a matter of perspective. We can see and you cannot, for you have not the vantage point. You would have to be beyond your world, outside the sphere of your world's influence, to see what we are seeing. And yet, to see what we see, we must remain hidden because if we were discovered, we would surely perish. For your visitors consider their mission here to be of the utmost value, and they consider the Earth to be their greatest prospect among several others. They will not stop because of us. So it is your own freedom that you must value and that you must defend. We cannot do this for you.

Every world, if it seeks to establish its own unity, freedom and self-determination in the Greater Community, must establish this freedom and defend it if necessary. Otherwise, domination will certainly occur and will be complete.

Why do your visitors want your world? It is so very obvious. It is not you they are interested in particularly. It is the biological resources of your world. It is the strategic position of this solar system. You are useful to them only insofar as these things are valued and can be utilized. They will offer what you want and they will speak what you want to hear. They will offer inducements, and they will use your religions and your religious ideals to foster confidence and trust that they, more than you, understand the needs of your world and will be able to serve these needs to bring about a greater equanimity here. Because humanity seems incapable of establishing unity and order, many people will open their minds and their hearts to those whom they believe will have the greater possibility for doing so.

Humanity has great promise and has cultivated a rich spiritual heritage, but it is without education regarding the Greater Community into which it is emerging.

In the second discourse, we spoke briefly of the interbreeding program. Some have heard of this phenomenon, and we understand there has been some discussion about this. The Unseen Ones have told us that there is a growing awareness that such a program exists, but incredibly people cannot see the obvious implications, being so given to their preferences in the matter and so ill equipped to deal with what such an Intervention could mean. Clearly, an interbreeding program is an attempt to fuse humanity's adaptation to the physical world with the visitors' group mind and collective consciousness. Such offspring would be in a perfect position to provide the new leadership for humanity, a leadership that is born of the visitors' intentions and the visitors' campaign. These individuals would have blood relations in the world, and so others would be related to them and accepting of their presence. And yet their minds would not be with you, nor their hearts. And though they may feel sympathy for you in your condition and for what your condition may well turn out to be, they would not have the individual authority, not being trained in The Way of Knowledge and Insight themselves, to assist you or to resist the collective consciousness that has fostered them here and given them life.

You see, individual freedom is not valued by the visitors. They consider it reckless and irresponsible. They only understand their own collective consciousness, which they see as privileged and blessed. And yet they cannot access true spirituality, which is called Knowledge in the universe, for Knowledge is born of an individual's self-discovery and is brought into being through relationships of a high caliber. Neither of these phenomena are present in the visitors' social makeup. They cannot think for themselves. Their will is not theirs alone. And so naturally they cannot respect the prospects for developing these two great phenomena within your world, and they are certainly in no position to foster such things. They only seek conformity and allegiance. And the spiritual teachings that they will foster in the world will only serve to make humans compliant, open and unsuspecting in order to garner a trust that has never been earned.

We have seen these things before in other places. We have seen entire worlds fall under control of such collectives. There are many such collectives in the universe. Because such collectives deal with interplanetary trade and extend over vast regions, they adhere to a strict conformity without deviation. There is no individuality amongst them, at least not in any way that you could recognize.

We are not sure that we can give an example in your own world of what this could be like, but we have been told there are commercial interests that span cultures in your world, that wield tremendous power and yet are governed by only a few. This is perhaps a good analogy for what we are describing. However, what we are describing is so much more powerful, pervasive and well established than anything that you could offer in the world as a good example.

It is true of intelligent life everywhere that fear can be a destructive force. Yet fear serves one and only one purpose if it is perceived correctly and that is to inform you of the presence of danger. We are concerned, and that is the nature of our fear. We understand what is at risk. That is the nature of our concern. Your fear is born because you do not know what is occurring, so it is a destructive fear. It is a fear that cannot empower you or give you the perception that you need to comprehend what is occurring within your world. If you can become informed, then fear is transformed into concern and concern is transformed into constructive action. We know of no other way to describe this.

> . . . the spiritual teachings that they will foster in the world will only serve to make humans compliant, open and unsuspecting in order to garner a trust that has never been earned.

The interbreeding program is becoming very successful. Already there are those walking your Earth who are born of the visitors' consciousness and collective endeavor. They cannot reside here for long periods of time, but within only a few years, they will be able to dwell upon the surface of your world permanently. Such will be the perfection of their genetic engineering that they will seem only slightly different from you, more in their manner and in their presence than in their physical appearance, to such a point that they will likely go unnoticed and unrecognized. However, they will have greater mental faculties. And this will give them an advantage that you could not match unless you were trained in The Ways of Insight.

Such is the greater reality into which humanity is emerging—a universe filled with wonders and horrors, a universe of influence, a universe of competition, yet also a universe filled with Grace, much like your own world but infinitely greater. The Heaven that you seek is not here. However, the forces that you must contend with are. This is the greatest threshold that your race will ever face. Each of us in our group has faced this in our own respective worlds, and there has been a great deal of failure, with only some success. Races of beings who can maintain their freedom and insulation must become strong and united and will likely withdraw from Greater Community interactions to a very great degree in order to protect that freedom.

> . . . fear serves one and only one purpose if it is perceived correctly and that is to inform you of the presence of danger.

If you think of these things, perhaps you will see corollaries in your own world. The Unseen Ones have told us a great deal regarding your spiritual development and its great promise, but they have also counseled us that your spiritual predispositions and ideals are being greatly manipulated at this time. There are entire teachings being introduced into the world now that teach human acquiescence and the suspension of critical abilities and value only that which is pleasurable and comfortable. These teachings are given to disable people's ability to access Knowledge within themselves until people reach a point where they feel they are completely dependent upon greater forces that they cannot identify. At that point, they will follow whatever is given them to do, and even if they sense something is wrong, they will no longer have the power to resist.

Humanity has lived in isolation for a long time. Perhaps it is believed that such an Intervention cannot possibly take place and that each person has proprietary rights over his or her own consciousness and mind. But these are only assumptions. Yet we have been told that the wise in your world have learned to overcome these assumptions and have gained the strength to establish their own mental environment.

We fear that our words may be too late and have too little impact and that the one we chose to receive us has too little assistance and support to make this information available. He will encounter disbelief and ridicule, for he will not be believed, and what he will speak of will contradict what many assume to be true. Those who have fallen under alien persuasion, they in particular will oppose him, for they have no choice in the matter.

Into this grave situation the Creator of all life has sent a preparation, a teaching of spiritual ability and discernment, power and accomplishment. We are students of such a teaching, as are many throughout the universe. This teaching is a form of Divine intervention. It does not belong to any one world. It is not the property of any one race. It is not centered around any hero or heroine, any one individual. Such a preparation is now available. It will be needed. From our perspective, it is the only thing currently that can give humanity an opportunity to become wise and discerning regarding your new life in the Greater Community.

As has occurred in your world in your own history, the first to reach the new lands are the explorers and the conquerors. They do not come for altruistic reasons. They come seeking power, resources and dominion. This is the nature of life. If humanity were well versed in Greater Community affairs, you would resist any visitation to your world unless a mutual agreement had been established previously. You would know enough not to allow your world to be so vulnerable.

> If humanity were well versed in Greater Community affairs, you would resist any visitation to your world unless a mutual agreement had been established previously. You would know enough not to allow your world to be vulnerable.

At this time, there is more than one collective competing for advantage here. That places humanity in the middle of a very unusual and yet enlightening set of circumstances. That is why the messages of the visitors will often seem inconsistent. There has been conflict amongst them, yet they will negotiate with each other should mutual benefit be recognized. However, they are still in competition. To them, this is the frontier. To them, you are only valued as being useful. If you are no longer recognized as being useful, you will simply be discarded.

Here there is a great challenge for the people of your world and particularly for those who are in positions of power and responsibility to recognize the difference between a spiritual presence and a visitation from the Greater Community. Yet how can you have the framework to make this distinction? Where can you learn such things? Who in your world is in the position to teach about the reality of the Greater Community? Only a teaching from beyond the world can prepare you for life beyond the world, and life beyond the world is now *in* your world, seeking to establish itself here, seeking to extend its influence, seeking to win the minds and hearts and souls of people everywhere. It is so simple. And yet so devastating.

Therefore, our task in these messages is to bring a great warning, but the warning is not enough. There must be a recognition amongst your people. At least amongst enough people here, there must be an understanding of the reality that you are now facing. This is the greatest event in human history—the greatest threat to human freedom and the greatest opportunity for human unity and cooperation. We recognize these great advantages and possibilities, but with each passing day their promise fades—as more and more people are captured and their awareness is recultivated and reconstituted, as more and more people learn of the spiritual teachings that are being promoted by the visitors and as more and more people become more acquiescent and less able to discern.

We have come at the request of the Unseen Ones to serve in this capacity as observers. Should we be successful, we will remain in the proximity of your world only long enough to continue to give you this information. Beyond that, we will return to our own homes. Should we fail and should the tide turn against humanity and should the great darkness come over the world, the darkness of domination, then we will have to depart, our mission unfulfilled. Either way, we cannot stay with you, though should you show promise we shall stay until you are safeguarded, until you can provide for yourselves. Included in this is the requirement that you be self-sufficient. Should you become reliant upon trade with other races, this creates a very great risk of manipulation from beyond, for humanity is not yet strong enough to resist the power in the mental environment that can be exerted here and is being exerted here now.

The visitors will try to create the impression that they are "the allies of humanity." They will say they are here to save humanity from itself, that only they can offer the great hope that humanity cannot provide for itself, that only they can establish true order and harmony in the world. But this order and this harmony will be theirs, not yours. And the freedom that they promise will not be yours to enjoy.

Manipulation of Religious Traditions and Beliefs

In order to understand the visitors' activities in the world today, we must present more information regarding their influence on world religious institutions and values and on the fundamental spiritual impulses which are common to your nature and which, in many ways, are common to intelligent life in many parts of the Greater Community.

We should begin by saying that the activities that the visitors are conducting in the world at this time have been carried on many times before in many different places with many different cultures in the Greater Community. Your visitors are not the originators of these activities but merely use them at their own discretion and have used them many times before.

It is important for you to understand that skills in influence and manipulation have been developed to a very high degree of functionality in the Greater Community. As races become more adept and more capable technologically, they exert more subtle and more pervasive kinds of influence upon one another. Human beings have only evolved thus far to compete with each other, so you do not yet have this adaptive advantage. This in itself is one of the reasons why we are presenting this material to you. You are entering a whole new set of circumstances that require the cultivation of your inherent abilities as well as the learning of new skills.

Though humanity represents a unique situation, emergence into the Greater Community has happened countless times before with other races. Therefore, what is being perpetrated upon you has been done before. It has been highly developed and is now being adapted to your life and to your situation with what we feel is relative ease.

The Pacification Program that is being implemented by the visitors is making this possible, in part. The desire for peaceful relations and the desire to avoid war and conflict are admirable but can be, and indeed *are* being, used against you. Even your most noble impulses can be used for other purposes. You have seen this in your own history, in your own nature and in your own societies. Peace can only be established upon a firm foundation of wisdom, cooperation and true ability.

Humanity has naturally been concerned with establishing peaceful relations amongst its own tribes and nations. Now, however, it has a greater set of problems and challenges. We view these as opportunities for your development, for it will only be the challenge of emerging into the Greater Community that will unite the world and give you the foundation for this unity to be genuine, strong and effective.

Therefore, we come not to criticize your religious institutions or your most fundamental impulses and values, but to illustrate how they are being used against you by those alien races who are intervening in your world. And, if it is within our power, we wish to encourage the right employment of your gifts and your accomplishments for the preservation of your world, your freedom and your integrity as a race within a Greater Community context.

The visitors are fundamentally practical in their approach. This is both a strength and a weakness. As we have observed them, both here and elsewhere, we see that it is difficult for them to deviate from their plans. They are not well adapted to change, nor can they deal with complexity very effectively. Therefore, they carry out their plan in an almost careless manner, for they feel that they are in the right and that they have the advantage. They do not believe that humanity will mount resistance against them—at least not resistance that will affect them greatly. And they feel that their secrets and their agenda are well preserved and are beyond human comprehension.

In this light, our activity in presenting this material to you makes us their enemies, certainly in their sight. In our sight, however, we are merely attempting to counter their influence and to give you the understanding that you need and the perspective that you must rely upon to preserve your freedom as a race and to deal with the realities of the Greater Community.

Due to the practical nature of their approach, they wish to accomplish their goals with the greatest efficiency possible. They wish to unite humanity but only in accordance with their own participation and activities in the world. To them, human unity is a practical concern. They do not value diversity in cultures; they certainly do not value it within their own cultures. Therefore, they will attempt to eradicate it or minimize it, if possible, wherever they are exerting their influence.

In our previous discourse, we talked about the visitors' influence on new forms of spirituality—on new ideas and new expressions of human divinity and human nature that are in your world at this time. In our discussion now, we would like to focus on the traditional values and institutions that your visitors seek to influence and are influencing today.

They do not value diversity in cultures; they certainly do not value it within their own cultures. Therefore, they will attempt to eradicate it or minimize it, if possible, wherever they are exerting their influence.

Attempting to promote uniformity and conformity, the visitors will rely on those institutions and those values that they feel are the most stable and practical for their use. They are not interested in your ideas, and they are not interested in your values, except insofar as these things might further their agenda. Do not deceive yourself in thinking that they are drawn to your spirituality because they lack such things themselves. This would be a foolish and perhaps fatal mistake. Do not think that they are enamored with your life and with those things that you find to be intriguing. For only in rare cases will you be able to influence them in this way. All natural curiosity has been bred out of them and very little remains. There is, in fact, very little of what you would call "Spirit" or what we would call "Varne" or "The Way of Insight." They are controlled and controlling and follow patterns of thinking and behavior that are firmly established and strictly reinforced. They might seem to empathize with your ideas, but it is only to gain your allegiance.

In traditional religious institutions in your world, they will seek to utilize those values and those fundamental beliefs that can serve in the future to bring you into allegiance to them. Let us give you some examples, born both of our own observations and of the insight that the Unseen Ones have given us over time.

Many in your world follow the Christian faith. We think this is admirable though it is certainly not the only approach to the fundamental questions of spiritual identity and purpose in life. The visitors will utilize the fundamental idea of allegiance to a single leader in order to generate allegiance to their cause. Within the context of this religion, the identification with Jesus the Christ will be greatly utilized. The hope and the promise of his return to the world offers your visitors a perfect opportunity, particularly at this turning point in the millennium.

It is our understanding that the true Jesus will not return to the world, for he is working in concert with the Unseen Ones and serves humanity and other races as well. The one who will come claiming his name will come from the Greater Community. He will be one who is born and bred for this purpose by the collectives that are in the world today. He will appear human and will have significant abilities compared to what you can accomplish at this moment. He will seem completely altruistic. He will be able to perform acts that will engender either fear or great reverence. He will be able to project images of angels, demons or whatever his superiors wish to expose you to. He will seem to have spiritual powers. Yet he will come from the Greater Community, and he will be part of the collective. And he will engender allegiance to follow him. Eventually, for those who cannot follow him, he will encourage their alienation or their destruction.

The visitors do not care how many of your people are destroyed so long as they have a primary allegiance amongst the majority.

Therefore, the visitors will focus on those fundamental ideas that give them this authority and influence.

A Second Coming, then, is being prepared by your visitors. The evidence of this, we understand, is already in the world. People do not realize the presence of the visitors or the nature of reality in the Greater Community, and so they will naturally accept their prior beliefs without question, feeling that the time has come for the great return of their Savior and their Teacher. But he who will come will not come from the Heavenly Host, he will not represent Knowledge or the Unseen Ones, and he will not represent the Creator or the Creator's will. We have seen this plan in formulation in the world. We have also seen similar plans carried out in other worlds.

In other religious traditions, uniformity will be encouraged by the visitors—what you might call a fundamental kind of religion based upon the past, based upon allegiance to authority and based upon conformity to the institution. This serves the visitors. They are not interested in the ideology and values of your religious traditions, only in their usefulness. The more that people can think alike, act alike and respond in predictable ways, the more useful they are to the collectives. This conformity is being promoted in many different traditions. The intent here is not to make them all the same but to have them be simple within themselves.

In one part of the world, one particular religious ideology will prevail; in a different part of the world, a different religious ideology will prevail. This is entirely useful to your visitors, for they do not care if there is more than one religion so long as there is order, conformity and allegiance. Having no religion of their own that you could possibly follow or identify with, they will use yours to engender their own values. For they value only total allegiance to their cause and to the collectives and seek your total allegiance to participate with them in ways that they prescribe. They will assure you that this will create peace and redemption in the world and the return of whatever religious image or personage is considered of the greatest value here.

This is not to say that fundamental religion is governed by alien forces, for we understand that fundamental religion has been well established in your world. What we are saying here is that the impulses for this and the mechanisms for this will be supported by the visitors and used for their own purposes. Therefore, great care must be given by all who are true believers in their traditions to discern these influences and to counteract them if possible. Here it is not the average person in the world that the visitors seek to convince; it is the leadership.

> Having no religion of their own that you could possible follow or identify with, they will use yours to engender their own values.

The visitors firmly believe that if they do not intervene in a timely manner, humanity will destroy itself and the world. This is not based upon truth; it is only an assumption. Though humanity is at risk of self-annihilation, this is not necessarily your destiny. But the collectives believe that this is so, and so they must act with haste and give their programs of persuasion great emphasis. Those who can be convinced will be valued as useful; those that cannot be convinced will be discarded and alienated. Should the visitors become strong enough to gain complete control of the world, those who cannot conform will simply be eliminated. Yet the visitors will not do the destruction. It will be wrought through the very individuals in the world who have fallen completely under their persuasion.

This is a terrible scenario, we understand, but there must be no confusion if you are to understand and receive what we are expressing in our messages to you. It is not the annihilation of humanity, it is the integration of humanity that the visitors seek to accomplish. They will interbreed with you for this purpose. They will attempt to redirect your religious impulses and institutions for this purpose. They will establish themselves in a clandestine manner in the world for this purpose. They will influence governments and government leaders for this purpose. They will influence military powers in the world for this purpose. The visitors are confident that they can be successful, for so far they see that humanity has not yet mounted enough resistance to counteract their measures or to offset their agenda.

> The visitors are confident that they can be successful, for so far they see that humanity has not yet mounted enough resistance to counteract their measures or to offset their agenda.

To counteract this, you must learn a Greater Community Way of Knowledge. Any free race in the universe must learn The Way of Knowledge, however it may be defined within their own cultures. This is the source of individual freedom. This is what enables individuals and societies to have true integrity and to have the wisdom necessary to deal with the influences that counteract Knowledge, both within their worlds and within the Greater Community. It is, therefore, necessary to learn new ways, for you are entering a new situation with new forces and new influences. Indeed, this is not some future prospect but an immediate challenge. Life in the universe does not wait upon your readiness. Events will happen whether you are prepared or not. Visitation has occurred without your agreement and without your permission. And your fundamental rights are being violated to a far greater degree than you yet realize.

Because of this, we have been sent not only to give our perspective and our encouragement but also to sound a calling, an alarm, to inspire an awareness and a commitment. We have said before that we cannot save your race through military intervention. That is not our role. And even if we attempted to do so and garnered the strength to carry out such an agenda, your world would be destroyed. We can only advise.

You will see in the future a ferocity of religious belief expressed in violent ways, carried out against people who disagree, against nations of less strength and used as a weapon of attack and destruction. The visitors would like nothing better than for your religious institutions to govern the nations. This you must resist. The visitors would like nothing better than to have religious values shared by everyone, for this adds to their labor force and makes their task easier. In all of its manifestations, such influence fundamentally reduces down to acquiescence and submission—submission of will, submission of purpose, submission of one's life and abilities. Yet this will be heralded as a great achievement for humanity, a great advancement in society, a new unification for the human race, a new hope for peace and equanimity, a triumph of human spirit over human instincts.

> The visitors would like nothing better than for your religious institutions to govern the nations. This you must resist.

Therefore, we come with our counsel and encourage you to refrain from making unwise decisions, from giving your life over to things that you do not understand and from acquiescing your discernment and your discretion for the sake of any promised reward. And we must encourage you not to betray Knowledge within yourself, the spiritual intelligence with which you were born and which now holds your only and greatest promise.

Perhaps in hearing this you will view the universe as a place devoid of Grace. Perhaps you will become cynical and afraid, thinking that avarice is universal. But this is not the case. What is needed now is for you to become strong, stronger than you are, stronger than you have been. Do not welcome communications with those intervening in your world until you have this strength. Do not open your minds and hearts to visitors from beyond the world, for they come here for their own purposes. Do not think that they will fulfill your religious prophesies or greatest ideals, for this is a delusion.

There are great spiritual forces in the Greater Community—individuals and even nations that have achieved very high states of accomplishment, far beyond what humanity has demonstrated thus far. But they do not come and take control of other worlds. They do not represent political and economic forces in the universe. They are not involved in commerce beyond fulfilling their own fundamental needs. They rarely travel, except in situations of emergency.

Emissaries are sent to help those who are emerging into the Greater Community, emissaries such as ourselves. And there are spiritual emissaries as well—the power of the Unseen Ones, who can speak to those who are ready to receive and who show good heart and good promise. This is how God works in the universe.

You are entering a difficult new environment. Your world is very valuable to others. You will need to protect it. You will need to preserve your resources so that you do not require or depend upon trade with other nations for the fundamental necessities of your life. If you do not preserve your resources, you will have to relinquish much of your freedom and self-sufficiency.

Your spirituality must be sound. It must be based upon real experience, for values and beliefs, rituals and traditions can be used and are being used by your visitors for their own purpose.

Here you can begin to see that your visitors are very vulnerable in certain areas. Let us explore this further. Individually, they have very little will and have difficulty dealing with complexities. They do not understand your spiritual nature. And they most certainly do not understand the impulses of Knowledge. The stronger you are with Knowledge, the more inexplicable you become, the harder you are to control and the less useful you become to them and to their program of integration. Individually, the stronger you are with Knowledge, the greater challenge you become to them. The more individuals that become strong with Knowledge, the more difficult it is for the visitors to isolate them.

The visitors do not have physical strength. Their power is in the mental environment and in the use of their technologies. Their numbers are small compared to yours. They are wholly reliant upon your acquiescence, and they are overly confident that they can succeed. Based upon their experience so far, humanity has not offered significant resistance. Yet the stronger you are with Knowledge, the more you become a force that opposes intervention and manipulation and the more you become a force for freedom and integrity for your race.

Though perhaps not many will be able to hear our message, your response is important. Perhaps it is easy to disbelieve our presence and our reality and to react against our message, yet we speak in accordance with Knowledge. Therefore, what we are saying can be known within you, if you are free to know it.

We understand that we challenge many beliefs and conventions in our presentation. Even our appearance here will seem inexplicable and will be rejected by many. Yet our words and our message can resonate with you because we speak with Knowledge. The power of truth is the greatest power in the universe. It has the power to free. It has the power to enlighten. And it has the power to give strength and confidence to those who need it.

. . . the stronger you are with Knowledge, the more you become a force that opposes intervention and manipulation and the more you become a force for freedom and integrity for your race.

We are told that human conscience is highly valued though perhaps not always followed. It is this that we are speaking of when we talk about The Way of Knowledge. It is fundamental to all of your true spiritual impulses. It is contained in your religions already. It is not new to you. But it must be valued, or our efforts and the efforts of the Unseen Ones to prepare humanity for the Greater Community will not be successful. Too few will respond. And the truth will be a burden for them, for they will not be able to share it effectively.

Therefore, we come not to criticize your religious institutions or conventions, but only to illustrate how they can be used against you. We are not here to replace them or to deny them, but to show how true integrity must pervade these institutions and conventions in order for them to serve you in a genuine way.

In the Greater Community, spirituality is embodied in what we call Knowledge, Knowledge meaning the intelligence of Spirit and the movement of Spirit within you. This empowers you to know rather than only believe. This gives you immunity from persuasion and manipulation, for Knowledge cannot be manipulated by any worldly power or force. This gives life to your religions and hope for your destiny.

We hold true to these ideas, for they are fundamental. They are lacking in the collectives, however, and should you encounter the collectives, or even their presence, and have the power to maintain your own mind, you will see this for yourself.

We are told that there are many people in the world who wish to give themselves over, to give themselves away to a greater power in life. This is not unique to the world of humanity, but in the Greater Community such an approach leads to enslavement. We understand that in your own world, before the visitors were here in such numbers, such an approach often led to enslavement. But in the Greater Community, you are more vulnerable and must be wiser, more careful and more self-sufficient. Recklessness here brings with it a heavy price and great misfortune.

> The power of truth is the greatest power in the universe. It has the power to free. It has the power to enlighten. And it has the power to give strength and confidence to those who need it.

If you can respond to Knowledge and learn a Greater Community Way of Knowledge, you will be able to see these things for yourself. Then you will confirm our words rather than only believe them or deny them. The Creator is making this possible, for the Creator wills that humanity prepare for its future. That is why we have come. That is why we are watching and now have the opportunity to report what we see.

The religious traditions of the world speak well for you in their essential teachings. We have had the opportunity to learn about them from the Unseen Ones. But they also represent a potential weakness. If humanity were more vigilant and understood the realities of life in the Greater Community and the meaning of premature visitation, your risks would not be so great as they are today. There is hope and expectation that such visitation will bring great rewards and will be a fulfillment for you. Yet you have not been able to learn of the reality of the Greater Community or of the powerful forces that are interacting with your world. Your lack of understanding and premature trust in the visitors do not serve you.

It is for this reason that the wise throughout the Greater Community remain hidden. They do not seek commerce in the Greater Community. They do not seek to be part of guilds or trading cooperatives. They do not seek diplomacy with many worlds. Their network of allegiance is more mysterious, more spiritual in nature. They understand the risks and the difficulties of exposure to the realities of life in the physical universe. They maintain their insulation, and they remain vigilant at their borders. They only seek to extend their wisdom through means that are less physical in nature.

In your own world, perhaps, you can see this expressed in those who are the wisest, the most gifted, who do not seek personal advantage through commercial avenues and who are not given to conquest and manipulation. Your own world tells you so much. Your own history tells you so much and illustrates, though on a smaller scale, everything that we are presenting to you here.

Thus, it is our intention not only to warn you of the gravity of your situation but to provide you, if we can, a greater perception and understanding of life, which you will need. And we trust that there will be enough who can hear these words and respond to the greatness of Knowledge. We hope there will be those who can recognize that our messages are not here to evoke fear and panic but to engender responsibility and a commitment to the preservation of freedom and good within your world.

If humanity should fail in opposing the Intervention, we can paint a picture of what this would mean. We have seen it elsewhere, for each one of us came very close, within our own worlds. Being part of a collective, the planet Earth will be mined for its resources, its people will be corralled to work and its rebels and heretics will be either alienated or destroyed. The world will be preserved for its agriculture and its mining interests. Human societies will exist, but only in subordination to powers from beyond your world. And should the world exhaust its usefulness, should its resources be completely taken, then you will be left, bereft. The supportive life upon your world will have been taken from you; the very means of survival will have been stolen. This has happened before in many other places.

In the case of this world, the collectives may choose to preserve the world for ongoing use as a strategic post and as a biological storehouse. Yet the human population would suffer terribly under such oppressive rule. The population of humanity would be reduced. The management of humanity would be given to those who are bred to lead the human race within a new order. Human freedom as you know it would no longer exist, and you would suffer under the weight of foreign rule, a rule that would be harsh and exacting.

There are many collectives in the Greater Community. Some of them are large; some of them are small. Some of them are more ethical in their tactics; many are not. To the extent that they compete with one another for opportunities, such as the rule of your world, dangerous activities can be perpetrated. We must give this illustration so that you will have no doubt as to what we are saying. The choices before you are very limited, but very fundamental.

Therefore, understand that from your visitors' perspective, you are all tribes that need to be managed and controlled in order to serve the visitors' interests. For this, your religions and a certain degree of your social reality will be preserved. But you will lose a great deal. And much will be lost before you realize what has been taken from you. Therefore, we can only advocate a vigilance, a responsibility and a commitment to learn—to learn about life in the Greater Community, to learn how to preserve your own culture and your own reality within a greater environment and to learn how to see who is here to serve you and distinguish them from those who are not. This greater discernment is so needed in the world, even for the resolution of your own difficulties. But regarding your survival and well-being in the Greater Community, it is absolutely fundamental.

Therefore, we encourage you to take heart. We have more to share with you.

Threshold:
A New Promise
for Humanity

In order to prepare for the alien presence that is in the world, it is necessary to learn more about life in the Greater Community, life that will envelope your world in the future, life that you will be a part of.

Humanity's destiny was always to emerge into a Greater Community of intelligent life. This is inevitable and occurs in all worlds where intelligent life has been seeded and has developed. Eventually, you would have come to realize that you lived within a Greater Community. And, eventually, you would have found that you were not alone in your own world, that visitation was occurring and that you would have to learn to contend with divergent races, forces, beliefs and attitudes that are prevalent in the Greater Community in which you live.

Emerging into the Greater Community is your destiny. Your isolation is now over. Though your world has been visited many times in the past, your isolated state has come to an end. Now it is necessary for you to reaize that you are no longer alone—in the universe or even within your own world. This understanding is presented more fully in the Teaching in Greater Community Spirituality that is being presented in the world today. Our role here is to describe life as it exists in the Greater Community so that you may have a deeper understanding of the greater panorama of life into which you are emerging. This is necessary in order for you to be able to approach this new reality with greater objectivity, understanding and wisdom. Humanity has lived in relative isolation for so long that it is natural for you to consider that the rest of the universe functions according to the ideas, principles and science that you hold sacred and upon which you base your activities and your perceptions of the world.

> The Greater Community is vast. Its furthest reaches have never been explored. It is greater than any race can comprehend. Within this magnificent creation, intelligent life exists at all levels of evolution and in countless expressions.

The Greater Community is vast. Its furthest reaches have never been explored. It is greater than any race can comprehend. Within this magnificent creation, intelligent life exists at all levels of evolution and in countless expressions. Your world exists in a part of the Greater Community that is fairly well inhabited. There are many areas of the Greater Community that have never been explored and other areas where races live in secret. Everything exists in the Greater Community in terms of the manifestations of life. And though life as we have been describing it seems difficult and challenging, the Creator works everywhere, reclaiming the separated through Knowledge.

In the Greater Community, there can be no one religion, one ideology or one form of government that can be adapted to all races and all peoples. Therefore, when we speak of religion, we speak of the spirituality of Knowledge, for this is the power and presence of Knowledge that dwells in all intelligent life—within you, within your visitors and within other races that you will encounter in the future.

Thus, universal spirituality becomes a great focal point. It brings together the divergent understandings and ideas that are prevalent in your world and gives your own spiritual reality a shared foundation. Yet the study of Knowledge is not only edifying, it is essential for survival and advancement in the Greater Community. For you to be able to establish and sustain your freedom and independence in the Greater Community, you must have this greater ability developed amongst enough people in your world. Knowledge is the only part of you that cannot be manipulated or influenced. It is the source of all wise understanding and action. It becomes a necessity within a Greater Community environment if freedom is valued and if you wish to establish your own destiny without being integrated into a collective or another society.

Therefore, while we present a grave situation in the world today, we also present a great gift and a great promise for humanity, for the Creator would not leave you unprepared for the Greater Community, which is the greatest of all thresholds that you as a race will face. We have been blessed with this gift as well. It has been in our possession for many of your centuries. We have had to learn it both out of choice and out of necessity.

> . . . when we speak of religion, we speak of the spirituality of Knowledge, for this is the power and presence of Knowledge that dwells in all intelligent life . . .

Indeed, it is the presence and the power of Knowledge which enables us to speak as your Allies and to provide the information that we are giving in these briefings. Had we never found this great Revelation, we would be isolated in our own worlds, unable to comprehend the greater forces in the universe which would shape our future and our destiny. For the gift that is being given in your world today has been given to us and to many other races as well who showed promise. This gift is especially important for emerging races such as your own who hold such promise and yet are so vulnerable in the Greater Community.

Therefore, while there can be no one religion or ideology in the universe, there is a universal principle, understanding and spiritual reality that is available to all. So complete is it that it can speak to those who are vastly different from you. It speaks to the diversity of life in all of its manifestations. You, living within your world, now have the opportunity to learn of such a great reality, to experience its power and grace for yourselves. Indeed, ultimately this is the gift that we wish to reinforce, for this will preserve your freedom and your self-determination and will open the door to a greater promise in the universe.

However, you have adversity and a great challenge at the outset. This requires you to learn a deeper Knowledge and a greater awareness. Should you respond to this challenge, you become the beneficiary not only for yourself, but for your entire race.

The teaching in Greater Community Spirituality is being presented in the world today. It has never been presented here before. It is being given through one person, who serves as the intermediary and speaker for this Tradition. It is being sent into the world at this critical time when humanity must learn of its life in the Greater Community and of the greater forces that are shaping the world today.

Only a teaching and understanding from beyond the world could give you this advantage and this preparation.

You are not alone in undertaking such a great task, for there are others in the universe undertaking this, even at your stage of development. You are but one of many races emerging into the Greater Community at this time. Each one holds promise and yet each is vulnerable to the difficulties, challenges and influences that exist in this greater environment. Indeed, many races have lost their freedom before it was ever attained only to become part of collectives or commercial guilds or client states to larger powers.

We do not wish to see this happen for humanity, for this would be a great loss. It is for this reason that we are here. It is for this reason that the Creator is active in the world today, bringing a new understanding to the human family. It is time for humanity to end its ceaseless conflicts with itself and to prepare for life in the Greater Community.

> It is time for humanity to end its ceaseless conflicts with itself and to prepare for life in the Greater Community.

You live in an area that has a great deal of activity beyond the sphere of your tiny solar system. Within this area, trade is carried on along certain avenues. Worlds interact, compete and sometimes conflict with each other. Opportunities are being sought by all who have commercial interests. They seek not only resources but also allegiances from worlds such as your own. Some are part of larger collectives. Others maintain their own alliances on a much smaller scale. Worlds that are able to emerge into the Greater Community successfully have had to maintain their autonomy and self-sufficiency to a great degree. This frees them from exposure to other forces which would only serve to exploit and manipulate them.

It is indeed your self-sufficiency and the development of your understanding and unity that become most essential for your well-being in the future. And this future is not far off, for already the influence of the visitors is becoming greater in your world. Many individuals have acquiesced to them already and now serve as their emissaries and intermediaries. Many other individuals simply serve as resources for their genetic program. This has happened, as we have said, many times in many places. It is not a mystery to us though it must seem incomprehensible to you.

The Intervention is both a misfortune and a vital opportunity. If you are able to respond, if you are able to prepare, if you are able to learn Greater Community Knowledge and Wisdom, then you will be able to offset the forces that are interfering in your world and build the foundation for greater unity amongst your own peoples and tribes. We, of course, encourage this, for this strengthens the bond of Knowledge everywhere.

In the Greater Community, warfare on a large scale rarely occurs. There are constraining forces. For one thing, warfare disturbs commerce and resource development. As a result, large nations are not allowed to act recklessly, for it impedes or offsets the goals of other parties, other nations and other interests. Civil war occurs periodically in worlds, but large-scale warfare between societies and between worlds is rare indeed. It is partly for this reason that skill in the mental environment has been established, for nations do compete with each other and attempt to influence one another. Since no one wants to destroy resources and opportunities, these greater skills and capabilities are cultivated with

...there is promise that you may be able to advance in this greater understanding and thus secure your freedom and preserve it.

varying degrees of success amongst many societies in the Greater Community. When these kinds of influences are present, the need for Knowledge is even greater.

Humanity is ill prepared for this. Yet because of your rich spiritual heritage and the degree to which personal freedom exists in your world today, there is promise that you may be able to advance in this greater understanding and thus secure your freedom and preserve it.

There are other constraints against warfare in the Greater Community. Most trading societies belong to large guilds that have established laws and codes of conduct for their members. These serve to constrain the activities of many who would seek to use force to gain access to other worlds and their proprietary resources. For warfare to break out on a large scale, many races would have to be involved, and this does not happen often. We understand that humanity is very warlike and conceives of conflict in the Greater Community in terms of warfare, but in reality you will find that this is not well tolerated and that other avenues of persuasion are employed in place of force.

Thus, your visitors come to your world not with great armaments. They do not come bringing large military forces, for they employ the skills that have served them in other ways—skills in manipulating the thoughts, the impulses and the feelings of those whom they encounter. Humanity is very vulnerable to such persuasions given the degree of superstition, conflict and mistrust that are prevalent in your world at this time.

Therefore, to understand your visitors and to understand others whom you will encounter in the future, you must establish a more mature approach to the use of power and influence. This is a vital part of your Greater Community education. Part of the preparation for this will be given in the Teaching in Greater Community Spirituality, but you must also learn through direct experience.

At present, we understand, there is a very fanciful view of the Greater Community amongst many people. It is believed that those who are technologically advanced are spiritually advanced as well, yet we can assure you that this is not the case. You yourselves, though more technologically advanced now than you were previously, have not spiritually advanced to a very great degree. You have more power, but with power comes the need for greater restraint.

> We understand that humanity is very warlike and conceives of conflict in the Greater Community in terms of warfare, but in reality you will find that this is not well tolerated and that other avenues of persuasion are employed in place of force.

There are those in the Greater Community who have far more power than you at a technological level and even at the level of thought. You will evolve to deal with them, but weaponry will not be your focus. For warfare on an interplanetary scale is so destructive that everyone loses. What are the spoils of such a conflict? What advantages does it secure? Indeed, when such conflict does exist, it happens in space itself and rarely in terrestrial environments. Rogue nations and those who are destructive and aggressive are quickly countered, particularly if they exist in well-populated areas where commerce is carried on.

Therefore, it is necessary for you to understand the nature of conflict in the universe because this will give you insight into the visitors and their needs—why they function the way they do, why individual freedom is unknown amongst them and why they rely upon their collectives. This gives them stability and power, but it also renders them vulnerable to those who are skilled with Knowledge.

Knowledge enables you to think in any number of ways, to act spontaneously, to perceive reality beyond the obvious and to experience the future and the past. Such abilities are beyond the reach of those who can only follow the regimens and the dictates of their cultures. You are far behind the visitors technologically, but you have the promise to develop skills in The Way of Knowledge, skills which you will need and must learn to rely upon increasingly.

We would not be the Allies of Humanity if we did not teach you about life in the Greater Community. We have seen much. We have encountered many different things. Our worlds were overcome and we had to regain our freedom. We know, from error and from experience, the nature of the conflict and the challenge that you face today. That is why we are well suited for this mission in our service to you. However, you will not meet us, and we will not come to meet the leaders of your nations. That is not our purpose.

> Knowledge enables you to think in any number of ways, to act spontaneously, to perceive reality beyond the obvious and to experience the future and the past.

Indeed, you need as little interference as possible, but you do need great assistance. There are new skills that you must develop and a new understanding that you must gain. Even a benevolent society, should they come to your world, would have such an influence and such an impact upon you that you would become dependent upon them and would not establish your own strength, your own power and your own self-sufficiency. You would be so reliant upon their technology and upon their understanding that they would not be able to leave you. And indeed, their arrival here would make you even more vulnerable to interference in the future. For you would desire their technology, and you would want to travel along the corridors of trade in the Greater Community. Yet you would not be prepared, and you would not be wise.

That is why your future friends are not here. That is why they are not coming to help you. For you would not become strong if they did. You would want to associate with them, you would want to have alliances with them, but you would be so weak that you could not protect yourselves. In essence, you would become part of their culture, which they do not will.

Even a benevolent society, should they come to your world, woud have such an influence and such an impact upon you that you would become dependent upon them . . .

Perhaps many people will not be able to understand what we are saying here, but in time this will make perfect sense to you, and you will see its wisdom and its necessity. At this moment, you are far too frail, too distracted and too conflicted to form strong alliances, even with those who could be your future friends. Humanity cannot yet speak as one voice, and so you are prone to intervention and manipulation from beyond.

As the reality of the Greater Community becomes more well known within your world, and if our message can reach enough people, then there will be a growing consensus that there is a greater problem facing humanity. This could create a new basis for cooperation and consensus. For what possible advantage can one nation in your world have over another when the entire world is threatened by the Intervention? And who could seek to gain individual power in an environment where alien forces are intervening? If freedom is to be real in your world, it must be shared. It must be recognized and known. It cannot be the privilege of the few or there will be no real strength here.

We understand from the Unseen Ones that already there are people who seek world dominion because they believe they have the visitors' blessings and support. They have the visitors' assurance that they will be assisted in their quest for power. And yet, what are they giving away but the keys to their own freedom and the freedom of their world? They are unknowing and unwise. They cannot see their error.

We also understand that there are those who believe that the visitors are here to represent a spiritual renaissance and a new hope for humanity, but how can they know, they who know nothing of the Greater Community? It is their hope and their desire that this be the case, and such wishes are accommodated by the visitors, for very obvious reasons.

As the reality of the Greater Community becomes more well known within your world, and if our message can reach enough people, then there will be a growing consensus that there is a greater problem facing humanity.

What we are saying here is there can be nothing short of real freedom in the world, real power and real unity. We make our message available to everyone, and we trust that our words can be received and considered seriously. Yet we have no control over your response. And the superstitions and the fears of the world may make our message beyond the reach for many. But the promise is still there. To give you more, we would have to take over your world, which we do not want to do. Therefore, we give all that we can give without interfering in your affairs. Yet there are many who want interference. They want to be rescued or saved by someone else. They do not trust the possibilities for humanity. They do not believe in humanity's inherent strengths and capabilities. They will give over their freedom willingly. They will believe what they are told by the visitors. And they will serve their new masters, thinking that what they are being given is their own liberation.

Freedom is a precious thing in the Greater Community. Never forget this. Your freedom, our freedom. And what is freedom but the ability to follow Knowledge, the reality that the Creator has given you, and to express Knowledge and to contribute Knowledge in all of its manifestations?

Your visitors do not have this freedom. It is unknown to them. They look at the chaos of your world, and they believe that the order that they will impose here will be redeeming for you and will save you from your own self-destruction. This is all they can give, for this is all that they have. And they will use you, but they do not consider this inappropriate, for they themselves are being used and know of no alternative to this. Their programming, their conditioning, is so thorough that to reach them at the level of their deeper spirituality holds only remote possibilities. You do not have the strength to do this. You would have to be so much stronger than you are today to have a redeeming influence on your visitors. And yet, their conformity is not so unusual in the Greater Community. It is very common in large collectives, where uniformity and compliance are essential to efficient functioning, particularly over vast areas of space.

Therefore, do not look at the Greater Community with fear, but with objectivity. The conditions that we are describing already exist in your world. You can understand these things. Manipulation is known to you. Influence is known to you. You have just never

> Freedom is a precious thing in the Greater Community. Never forget this. Your freedom, our freedom.

encountered them on such a great scale, nor have you ever had to compete with other forms of intelligent life. As a result, you do not yet have the skills to do so.

We speak of Knowledge because it is your greatest ability. Regardless of what technology you can develop over time, Knowledge is your greatest promise. You are far behind the visitors in your technological development, so you must rely upon Knowledge. It is the greatest force in the universe, and your visitors do not use it. It is your only hope. That is why the Teaching in Greater Community Spirituality teaches The Way of Knowledge, provides the *Steps to Knowledge* and teaches Greater Community Wisdom and Insight. Without this preparation, you would not have the skill or the perspective to understand your dilemma or to respond to it effectively. It is too big. It is too new. And you are not adapted to these new circumstances.

The visitors' influence is growing with each passing day. Every person who can hear this, feel this and know this must learn The Way of Knowledge, The Greater Community Way of Knowledge. This is a calling. It is a gift. It is a challenge.

Under more pleasant circumstances, well, the need may not seem as great. But the need is tremendous, for there is no security, there is no place to hide, there is no retreat in the world that is secure from the alien presence that is here. That is why there are only two choices: you can acquiesce or you can stand for your freedom.

> You are far behind the visitors in your technological development, so you must rely upon Knowledge. It is the greatest force in the universe, and your visitors do not use it. It is your only hope.

This is the great decision placed before each person. This is the great turning point. You cannot be foolish in the Greater Community. It is too demanding an environment. It requires excellence, commitment. Your world is too valuable. The resources here are coveted by others. The strategic position of your world is held in high regard. Even if you were living in some remote world far from any trade route, far from all commercial engagements, eventually you would be discovered by someone. That eventuality has come for you now. And it is well underway.

. . . there are only two choices: you can acquiesce or you can stand for your freedom.

Take heart, then. This is a time for courage, not for ambivalence. The gravity of the situation facing you only confirms the importance of your life and your response and the importance of the preparation that is being given in the world today. It is not only for your edification and advancement. It is for your protection and your survival as well.

Questions & Answers*

We feel that it is important, given the information that we have provided thus far, to respond to questions that must surely arise regarding our reality and the significance of the messages that we have come to give.

♦

"Given the lack of hard evidence, why should people believe what you are telling them about the Intervention?"

First, there must be great evidence concerning the visitation to your world. We have been told that this is the case. Yet we have also been told by the Unseen Ones that people do not know how to understand the evidence and that they give it their own meaning—a meaning that they prefer to give it, a meaning that provides comfort and reassurance for the most part. We are certain that there is adequate evidence to verify that the Intervention is occur-

---

* These questions were sent to New Knowledge Library by many of the first readers of the Allies Material.

ring in the world today if one takes the time to look and to investigate this matter. The fact that your governments or religious leaders do not reveal such things does not mean that such a great event is not occurring in your midst.

◆

"How can people know that you are real?"

Regarding our reality, we cannot demonstrate our physical presence to you, and so you must discern the meaning and the import of our words. At this point, it is not merely a matter of belief. It requires a greater recognition, a Knowledge, a resonance. The words we speak we believe are true, but that does not assure that they can be received as such. We cannot control the response to our message. There are people who require more evidence than can possibly be given. For others, such evidence will not be necessary, for they will feel an inner confirmation.

> The words we speak we believe are true, but that does not assure that they can be received as such. We cannot control the response to our message.

In the meantime, perhaps we remain a controversy, and yet we hope and we trust that our words can be considered seriously and that the evidence that does exist, which is substantial, can be gathered and understood by those who are willing to give this their effort and their focus in life. From our perspective, there is no greater problem, challenge and opportunity to receive your attention.

Therefore, you are at the beginning of a new understanding. This does require faith and self-reliance. Many will reject our words simply because they do not believe that we could possibly exist.

Others perhaps will think that we are part of some manipulation that is being cast upon the world. We cannot control these responses. We can only reveal our message and our presence in your life, however removed that presence may be. It is not our presence here that is of paramount importance, but the message that we have come to reveal and the greater perspective and understanding that we can provide for you. Your education must begin somewhere. All education begins with the desire to know.

We hope that through our discourses we can gain at least part of your confidence in order to begin to reveal what we are here to offer.

◆

*"What do you have to say to those who view the
Intervention as a positive thing?"*

We understand, first of all, the expectation that all forces from the heavens are related to your spiritual understanding, traditions and fundamental beliefs. The idea that there is prosaic life in the universe is a challenge to these fundamental assumptions. From our perspective and given the experience of our own cultures, we understand these expectations. In the distant past, we maintained them ourselves. And yet we had to relinquish them in facing the realities of Greater Community life and the meaning of visitation.

You live in a great physical universe. It is full of life. This life represents countless manifestations and also represents the evolution of intelligence and spiritual awareness at every level. What this means is that what you will encounter in the Greater Community encompasses almost every possibility.

However, you are isolated and do not yet travel in space. And even if you had the capability to reach another world, the universe is vast, and no one has gained the ability to go from one end of the galaxy to the other with any kind of speed. Therefore, the physical universe remains enormous and incomprehensible. No one has mastered its laws. No one has conquered its territories. No one can claim complete dominance or control. Life has a great humbling effect in this way. Even far beyond your borders this is true.

. . . what you will encounter in the Greater Community encompasses almost every possibility.

You should then come to expect that you will meet intelligences representing forces for good, forces for ignorance and those who are more neutral regarding you. However, in the realities of Greater Community travel and exploration, emerging races such as your own will, almost without exception, encounter resource explorers, collectives and those seeking advantage for themselves as their first contact with Greater Community life.

Regarding the positive interpretation of visitation, part of this is human expectation and the natural desire to welcome a good outcome and to seek help from the Greater Community for the problems that humanity has not been able to resolve on its own. It is normal to expect such things, particularly when you are considering that your visitors have greater capabilities than do you. However, a large part of the problem in interpreting the great visitation has to do with the will and the agenda of the visitors themselves. For they are encouraging people everywhere to view their presence here as wholly beneficial to humanity and to its needs.

♦

*"If this Intervention is so well underway, why didn't you
come sooner?"*

At an earlier time, many years ago, several groups of your allies came to your world to visit in an attempt to give a message of hope, to prepare humanity. But alas their messages could not be understood and were misused by those few who could receive them. In the wake of their coming, the visitors from the collectives have amassed and gathered here. It has been known to us that this would happen, for your world is far too valuable to be overlooked, and, as we have said, it does not exist in a remote and distant part of the universe. Your world has been observed for a long time by those who would seek to use it for their own benefit.

♦

"Why can't our allies stop the Intervention?"

We are only here to observe and to advise. The great decisions facing humanity are in your hands. No one else can make these decisions for you. Even your great friends far beyond your world would not intervene, for if they did so, it would cause warfare, and your world would become a battleground between opposing forces. And should your friends be victorious, you would become wholly reliant upon them, unable to fend for yourself or to maintain your own security in the universe. We know of no benevolent race that would seek to bear this burden. And, in truth, it would not serve you either.

For you would become a client state to another power and would have to be governed from afar. This is not beneficial for you in any way, and it is for this reason that this is not occurring. Yet the visitors will cast themselves as saviors and rescuers of humanity. They will utilize your naiveté. They will capitalize on your expectations, and they will seek to wholly benefit from your trust.

The great decisions facing humanity are in your hands. No one else can make these decisions for you.

Therefore, it is our sincere desire that our words can serve as an antidote to their presence and to their manipulation and abuse. For your rights are being violated. Your territory is being infiltrated. Your governments are being persuaded. And your religious ideologies and impulses are being redirected.

There must be a voice of truth regarding this. And we can only trust that you can receive this voice of truth. We can only hope that the persuasion has not gone too far.

♦

"What are realistic goals for us to set, and what is the
bottom line with regard to saving humanity from
losing its self-determination?"

The first step is awareness. Many people must become aware that the Earth is being visited and that foreign powers are here operating in a clandestine manner, seeking to hide their agenda and endeavors from human understanding. It must be very clear that their presence here is a great challenge to human freedom and self-determination. The agenda that they are furthering and the Pacification Program that they are sponsoring must be countered with sobriety and wisdom regarding their presence. This counteraction must occur. There are many people in the world today who are able to understand this. Therefore, the first step is awareness.

The next step is education. It is necessary for many people in different cultures and in different nations to learn about life in the Greater Community and to begin to comprehend what you will be dealing with and are dealing with even at this moment.

Therefore, realistic goals are awareness and education. This in itself would obstruct the visitors' agenda in the world. They are operating now with very little resistance. They are encountering few obstacles. All those who seek to view them as "allies of humanity" must learn that this is not the case. Perhaps our words will not be enough, but they are a beginning.

...realistic goals are awareness and education. This in itself would obstruct the visitors' agenda in the world. They are operating now with very little resistance.

◆

"Where can we find this education?"

The education can be found in The Greater Community Way of Knowledge, which is being presented in the world at this time. Though it presents a new understanding about life and spirituality in the universe, it is connected to all of the genuine spiritual paths that already exist within your world—spiritual paths that value human freedom and the meaning of true spirituality and that value cooperation, peace and harmony within the human family. Therefore, the teaching in The Way of Knowledge calls forth all the great truths that already exist in your world and gives them a greater context and arena of expression. In this way, The Greater Community Way of Knowledge does not replace the world's religions, but provides a larger context within which they can be truly meaningful and relevant to your times.

◆

"How do we convey your message to others?"

The truth lives within each person at this moment. If you can speak to the truth in a person, it will become stronger and begin to resonate. Our great hope, the hope of the Unseen Ones, the spiritual forces who serve your world, and the hope of those who value human freedom and wish to see your emergence into the Greater Community successfully fulfilled, rely upon this truth that lives within each person. We cannot force this awareness upon you. We can only reveal it to you and trust in the greatness of Knowledge that the Creator has given you that can enable you and others to respond.

> The truth lives within each person at this moment. If you can speak to the truth in a person, it will become stronger and begin to resonate.

◆

"Where do humanity's strengths lie in opposing the Intervention?"

First, we understand from observing your world, and from what the Unseen Ones have told us regarding things that we cannot see, that though there are great problems within the world, there is sufficient human freedom to give you a foundation for opposing the

Intervention. This is in contrast to many other worlds where individual freedom was never established to begin with. As these worlds encounter alien forces in their midst and the reality of Greater Community life, the possibility for them to establish freedom and independence is very limited.

Therefore, you have a great strength in that human freedom is known in your world and is valued by many, though perhaps not all. You know you have something to lose. You value what you have already, to whatever extent it has been established. You do not want to be ruled by foreign powers. You do not even want to be ruled harshly by human authorities. Therefore, this is a beginning.

Next, because your world has rich spiritual traditions that have fostered Knowledge in the individual and fostered human cooperation and understanding, the reality of Knowledge has already been established. Again, in other worlds where Knowledge was never established, the possibility for establishing it at the turning point of emerging into the Greater Community shows little hope for success. Knowledge is strong enough in enough people here that they may be able to learn of the reality of life in the Greater Community and to comprehend what is occurring in their midst at this time. It is for this reason that we are hopeful, for we trust in human wisdom. We trust that people can rise above selfishness, self-preoccupation and self-protection to view life in a greater way and to feel a greater responsibility in service to their own kind.

Perhaps our faith is unfounded, but we are trusting that the Unseen Ones have counseled us wisely regarding this. As a result, we have placed ourselves at risk by being in the proximity of your world and witnessing events beyond your borders that have direct bearing on your future and destiny.

Humanity has great promise. You have a growing awareness of problems in the world—the lack of cooperation amongst nations, the degradation of your natural environment, your diminishing resources and so forth. If these problems were unknown to your people, if these realities had been kept hidden from your people, to the extent that people had no idea of the existence of these things, then we would not be as hopeful. However, the reality remains that humanity has the potential and the promise to counteract any intervention into the world.

◆

"Is this Intervention going to become a military invasion?"

As we have said, your world is too valuable to incite a military invasion. No one who is visiting your world wants to destroy its infrastructure or its natural resources. That is why the visitors do not seek to destroy humanity, but instead to engage humanity in service to their collectives.

It is not military invasion that threatens you. It is the power of inducement and persuasion. This will be built upon your own weakness, upon your own selfishness, upon your ignorance of life in the Greater Community and upon your blind optimism regarding your future and the meaning of life beyond your borders.

It is not military invasion that threatens you. It is the power of inducement and persuasion.

To counteract this, we provide education and we speak of the means of preparation that are being sent into the world at this time. If you did not already know human freedom, if you were not already aware of the problems endemic to your world, then we could not entrust such a preparation to you. And we would not have confidence that our words would resonate with the truth of what you know.

♦

"Can you influence people as powerfully as the visitors, but for the good?"

Our intention is not to influence individuals. Our intention is only to present the problem and the reality into which you are emerging. The Unseen Ones are providing the actual means of preparation, for that comes from the Creator of all life. In this, the Unseen Ones influence individuals for the good. But there are restraints. As we have said, it is your self-determination that must be strengthened. It is your power that must be increased. It is your cooperation amongst the human family that must be supported.

There are limits as to how much help we can provide. Our group is small. We are not walking amongst you. Therefore, the great understanding of your new reality must be shared from person to person. It cannot be forced upon you from a foreign power, even if it were for your own good. We would not, then, be supporting your freedom and self-determination if we sponsored such a program of persuasion. Here you cannot be like children. You must become mature and responsible. It is your freedom that is at stake. It is your world that is at stake. It is your cooperation with each other that is needed.

You now have a great cause to unite your race, for none of you will benefit without the other. No nation will benefit if any other nation falls under alien control. Human freedom must be complete. The cooperation must occur around your world. For everyone is in the same situation now. The visitors do not favor one group over another, one race over another, one nation over another. They only seek the avenue of least resistance to establish their presence and their domination of your world.

◆

"How extensive is their infiltration of humanity?"

The visitors have a significant presence within the most advanced nations in your world, particularly the nations of Europe, Russia, Japan and the United States. These are viewed as the strongest nations, having the greatest power and influence. It is there that the visitors will concentrate. However, they are taking people from all over the world, and they are furthering their Pacification Program with all those that they capture, if those individuals can be responsive to their influence. Therefore, the visitors' presence is worldwide, but they are concentrating on those whom they hope will become their allies. These are the nations and governments and religious leaders who hold the greatest power and sway over human thought and conviction.

◆

"How much time do we have?"

How much time do you have? You have some time, how much

we cannot tell. But we come with an urgent message. This is not a problem that can simply be avoided or denied. From our perspective, it is the most important challenge facing humanity. It is of the greatest concern, the first priority. You are late in your preparation. This was caused by many factors beyond our control. But there is time, if you can respond. The outcome is uncertain and yet there is still hope for your success.

◆

"How can we focus on this Intervention given the
immensity of other global problems which are occurring
right now?"

First of all, we feel that there are no other problems in the world that are as important as this. From our perspective, whatever you can resolve on your own will have little meaning in the future if your freedom is lost. What could you hope to gain? What could you hope to achieve or secure if you are not free in the Greater Community? All of your accomplishments would be given to your new governors; all of your wealth would be bestowed upon them. And though your visitors are not cruel, they are completely committed to their agenda. You are valued only insofar as you can be useful to their cause. It is for this reason that we do not feel that there are any other problems facing humanity as important as this.

> What could you hope to achieve or secure if you are not free in the Greater Community?

♦

"Who is likely to respond to this situation?"

Regarding who can respond, there are many people in the world today who have an inherent knowledge of the Greater Community and who are sensitive to it. There are many others who have been taken by the visitors already but who have not yielded to them or to their persuasion. And there are many others who are concerned about the future of the world and who are alerted to the dangers that humanity faces. People in all or any of these three categories may be amongst the first to respond to the Greater Community reality and to the preparation for the Greater Community. They may come from any walk of life, from any nation, from any religious background or from any economic group. They are literally all over the world. It is upon them and upon their response that the great Spiritual Powers that protect and oversee human welfare are depending.

♦

The more you can become strong with Knowledge and aware of the visitors' presence, the less you become a desirable subject for their study and manipulation.

"You mention that individuals are being taken all over the world. How can people protect themselves or others from being abducted?"

The more you can become strong with Knowledge and aware of the visitors' presence, the less you become a desirable subject for their study and manipulation. The more you use your encounters with *them* to gain insight into them, the more of a hazard you become. As we have said, they seek the path of least resistance. They want individuals who are compliant and yielding. They want those who cause them few problems and little concern.

Yet as you become strong with Knowledge, you will be beyond their control because now they cannot capture your mind or your heart. And with time, you will have the power of perception to see into their minds, which they do not wish. You then become a danger to them, a challenge to them, and they will avoid you if they can.

The visitors do not want to be revealed. They do not wish for conflict. They are overly confident that they can achieve their goals without serious resistance from the human family. But once such resistance is mounted, once the power of Knowledge awakens in the individual, then the visitors are facing a much more formidable obstacle. Their intervention here becomes thwarted and more difficult to achieve. And their persuasion of those in power becomes more difficult to accomplish. Therefore, it is the individual's response and commitment to the truth that are essential here.

Become aware of the visitors' presence. Do not yield to the persuasion that their presence here is of a spiritual nature or that it holds great benefit or salvation for humanity. Resist the persuasion. Regain your own inner authority, the great gift that the Creator has given to you. Become a force to be reckoned with regarding any who would trespass against or deny your fundamental rights.

This is Spiritual Power being expressed. It is the Will of the Creator that humanity should emerge into the Greater Community united within itself and free from foreign intervention and domination. It is the Creator's Will that you should prepare for a future that will be unlike your past. We are here in service to the Creator, and thus our presence and our words serve this purpose.

◆

"If the visitors encounter resistance in humanity or in
*   certain individuals, will they come in greater numbers or*
*   will they leave?"*

Their numbers are not great. Should they encounter considerable resistance, they would have to fall back and make new plans. They are wholly confident that their mission can be fulfilled without serious obstacles. Yet should serious obstacles arise, then their intervention and persuasion would be thwarted, and they would have to find other ways of gaining contact with humanity.

> Their numbers are not great. Should they encounter considerable resistance, they would have to fall back and make new plans.

We trust that the human family can generate enough resistance and enough consensus in order to offset these influences. It is upon this that we are basing our hope and efforts.

◆

"What are the most important questions that we must ask
*   of ourselves and others with respect to this problem of alien*
*   infiltration?"*

Perhaps the most critical questions to ask yourself are, "Are we humans alone within the universe or in our own world? Are we being visited at this time? Is this visitation beneficial to us? Do we need to prepare?"

These are very fundamental questions, but they must be asked. There are many questions, however, that cannot be answered, for you do not know enough about life in the Greater Community, and you are not yet confident that you have the ability to counteract these influences. There are many things lacking in human education, which is primarily focused upon the past. Humanity is emerging from a long state of relative isolation. Its education, its values and its institutions were all established within this state of isolation. Yet your isolation now is over, forever. It was always known that this would happen. It was inevitable that this would be the case. Therefore, your education and your values are entering into a new context, to which they must adapt. And the adaptation must happen quickly because of the nature of the Intervention in the world today.

There will be many questions that you cannot answer. You will have to live with them. Your education about the Greater Community is only at the very beginning. You must approach it with great sobriety and care. You must counteract your own tendencies to try and make the situation pleasant or reassuring. You must develop an objectivity about life, and you must look beyond your own personal sphere of interests in order to put yourself in a position to respond to the greater forces and events that are shaping your world and your future.

Humanity is emerging from a long state of relative isolation.

◆

"What if enough people cannot respond?"

We are confident that enough people can respond and begin

their great education about life in the Greater Community in order to give promise and hope to the human family. If this cannot be achieved, then those who value their freedom and who have this education will have to retreat. They will have to keep Knowledge alive in the world as the world falls under complete control. This is a very grave alternative, and yet it has occurred in other worlds. The journey back to freedom from such a position is quite difficult. We hope that this will not be your fate, and that is why we are here giving you this information. As we have said, there are enough people in the world who can respond to offset the intentions of the visitors and to thwart their influence on human affairs and human values.

◆

"You speak of other worlds emerging into the Greater Community. Can you speak of successes and failures which might have bearing on our situation?"

There have been successes or we would not be here. In my case, as the speaker for our group, our world had already been greatly infiltrated before we realized the situation at hand. Our education was prompted by the arrival of a group such as ourselves, providing insight and information about our situation. We had alien resource traders in our world interacting with our government. Those who were in power at that time were persuaded that trade and commerce would be beneficial to us, for we were beginning to experience resource depletion. Though our race was united, unlike your own, we began to be wholly depen-

Though our race was united, unlike your own, we began to be wholly dependent upon the new technology and opportunities that were being presented to us.

dent upon the new technology and opportunities that were being presented to us. And yet as this occurred, there was a shift in the center of power. We were becoming the clients. The visitors were becoming the providers. As time went on, terms and restrictions were placed upon us, subtly at first.

Our religious focus and beliefs were also influenced by the visitors, who showed interest in our spiritual values but who wished to give us a new understanding, an understanding based upon the collective, based upon the cooperation of minds thinking alike in unison with each other. This was presented to our race as an expression of spirituality and achievement. Some were persuaded, and yet because we were well advised from our allies beyond our world, allies such as ourselves, we began to mount a resistance movement and over time were able to force the visitors to leave our world.

Since that time, we have learned a great deal about the Greater Community. The trade that we maintain is very selective, with only a few other nations. We have been able to avoid the collectives, and that has preserved our freedom. And yet our success was difficult to achieve, for there were many of us who had to die in the face of this conflict. Ours is a story of success, but not without cost. There are others in our group who have experienced similar difficulties in their interaction with intervening powers in the Greater Community. And yet because we eventually learned to travel beyond our borders, we gained alliance with one another. We were able to learn what spirituality means in the Greater Community. And the Unseen Ones, who serve our world as well, helped us in this regard to make the great transition from isolation to Greater Community awareness.

Yet there have been many failures that we are aware of. Cultures where the indigenous peoples had not established personal freedom or had not tasted the fruits of cooperation, even though they were advancing technologically, did not have a foundation to establish their own independence in the universe. Their ability to resist the collectives was very limited. Induced by promises of greater power, greater technology and greater wealth, and induced by the seeming benefits of trade in the Greater Community, their center of power left their world. In the end, they became wholly dependent upon those who supplied them and who gained control of their resources and their infrastructures.

Consider the peoples in your world who have lost their freedom because they lived in a place considered valuable by others. It is now the whole human family that is so imperiled.

Surely you can imagine how this could be the case. Even within your own world according to your history, you have seen smaller nations fall under the domination of greater ones. You can see this even today. Therefore, these ideas are not wholly foreign to you. In the Greater Community, as in your world, the strong will dominate the weak, if they can. This is a reality of life everywhere. And it is for this reason that we are encouraging your awareness and your preparation, in order that you may become strong and your self-determination may grow.

It may be a grave disappointment to many to understand and to learn that freedom is rare in the universe. As nations become stronger and more technological, they require greater and greater uniformity and compliance amongst their peoples. As they bridge out into the Greater Community and become involved in Greater Community affairs, the tolerance for individual expression diminishes to the point where large nations that have wealth and power are governed with a strictness and an exacting attitude that you would find abhorrent.

Here you must learn that technological advancement and spiritual advancement are not the same, a lesson that humanity has yet to learn and which you *must* learn if you are to exercise your natural wisdom in these matters.

Your world is greatly valued. It is rich biologically. You are sitting on a prize that you must protect if you are to be its stewards and its beneficiaries. Consider the peoples in your world who have lost their freedom because they lived in a place considered valuable by others. It is now the whole human family that is so imperiled.

◆

"Because the visitors are so skilled in projecting thoughts
and influencing people's mental environment, how do we
ensure ourselves that what we are seeing is real?"

The only basis for wise perception is the cultivation of Knowledge. If you believe only what you see, then you will believe only what is shown to you. There are many, we are told, that have this perspective. Yet we have learned that the wise everywhere must gain a greater vision and a greater discernment. It is true that your visitors can project images of your saints and of your religious figures. Though this is not practiced often, it certainly can be used in order to evoke commitment and dedication amongst those who are already given to such beliefs. Here your spirituality becomes an area of vulnerability where wisdom must be used.

Yet the Creator has given you Knowledge as a foundation for

true discernment. You can know what you are seeing if you ask your-self if it is real. Yet to do this, you must have this foundation, and that is why the teaching in The Way of Knowledge is so fundamental to learning Greater Community Spirituality. Without this, people will believe what they want to believe, and they will rely upon what they see and what they are shown. And their potential for freedom will have been lost already, for it was never allowed to flourish in the first place.

◆

"You speak about keeping Knowledge alive. How many will
it take to keep Knowledge alive in the world?"

We cannot give you a number, but it must be strong enough to generate a voice within your own cultures. If this message can only be received by a few, they will not have this voice or this strength. Here they must share their wisdom. It cannot be purely for their own edification. Many more must learn of this message, many more than can receive it today.

◆

"Is there a danger in presenting this message?"

There is always a danger in presenting the truth, not only in your world, but elsewhere. People gain advantage from the circum-stances as they currently exist. The visitors will offer advantage to those in power who can receive them and who are not strong in Knowledge. People become accustomed to these advantages and build their lives upon them. This makes them resistant or even hostile to the presentation of truth, which calls for their responsibility in service to others and which may threaten the basis of their wealth and achievements.

This is why we are hidden and do not walk in your world. Certainly the visitors would destroy us if they could find us. But humanity may seek to destroy us as well because of what we represent, because of the challenge and the new reality that we demonstrate. Not everyone is ready to receive the truth even though it is greatly needed.

> There is always a danger in presenting the truth, not only in your world, but elsewhere.

♦

"Can individuals who are strong with Knowledge influence
the visitors?"

The chance of success here is very limited. You are dealing with a collective of beings who have been bred to be compliant, whose whole life and experience have been encompassed and engendered by a collective mentality. They do not think for themselves. For this reason, we do not feel that you can influence them. There are few amongst the human family who have the strength to do this, and even here the possibility for success would be very limited. So the answer must be "No." For all practical purposes, you cannot win them over.

◆

"How are collectives different from a united humanity?"

Collectives are made up of different races and of those who are bred to serve those races. Many of the beings that are being encountered in the world are bred by collectives to be servants. Their genetic heritage has long been lost to them. They are bred to serve, as you breed animals to serve you. The human cooperation that we are promoting is a cooperation that preserves the self-determination of individuals and provides a position of strength from which humanity can interact, not only with the collectives but with others who will visit your shores in the future.

A collective is based upon one belief, one set of principles and one authority. Its emphasis is complete allegiance to an idea or an ideal. Not only is this engendered in the education of your visitors, but in their genetic code as well. That is why they behave in the ways that they do. This is both their strength and their weakness. They have great strength in the mental environment because their minds are united. But they are weak because they cannot think for themselves. They cannot deal with complexities or adversity very successfully. A man or woman of Knowledge would be incomprehensible to them.

Humanity must unite to preserve its freedom, but this is a very different establishment from the creation of a collective. We call them "collectives" because they are collectives of different races and nationalities. Collectives are not one race. Though there are many races in the Greater Community that are ruled by a dominant authority, a collective is an organization that spans beyond the allegiance of one race to its own world.

Collectives can have great power. Yet because there are many collectives, they tend to compete with one another, which prevents any one of them from becoming dominant. Also, various nations in the Greater Community have long-standing disputes with one another, which are difficult to bridge. Perhaps they have competed for a long time for the same resources. Perhaps they compete with one another to sell the resources that they have. Yet a collective is a different matter. As we are saying here, it is not based upon one race and one world. They are the result of conquest and domination. That is why your visitors are comprised of different races of beings at different levels of authority and command.

◆

"In other worlds that have successfully unified, did they maintain their individual freedom of thought?"

To varying degrees. Some to a very high degree, others less so, depending upon their history, their psychological make-up and the needs of their own survival. Your life in the world has been relatively easy compared to where other races have developed. Most places where intelligent life exists have been colonized, for there are not many terrestrial planets such as your own that provide such a wealth of biological resources. Their freedom, in large part, depended upon the wealth of their environments. But they have all been successful in thwarting alien infiltration and have established their own lines of trade, commerce and communication based upon their own self-determination. This is a rare accomplishment and must be earned and protected.

◆

"What will it take to achieve human unity?"

Humanity is very vulnerable in the Greater Community. This vulnerability, in time, can foster a fundamental cooperation amongst the human family, for you must join and unite in order to survive and to advance. This is part of having a Greater Community awareness. If this is based upon the principles of human contribution, freedom and self-expression, then your self-sufficiency can become very strong and very rich. But there must be greater cooperation in the world. People cannot live for themselves alone or put their own personal goals above and beyond the needs of everyone else. Some may view this as a loss of freedom. We see it as a guarantee for future freedom. For given the current attitudes prevalent in the world today, your future freedom would be very difficult to secure or maintain. Take heed. Those who are driven by their own selfishness are the perfect candidates for foreign influence and manipulation. If they are in positions of power, they will give over their nation's wealth, their nation's freedom and their nation's resources in order to gain advantage for themselves.

Therefore, greater cooperation is required. Surely you can see this. Surely this is apparent even within your own world. But this is very different from the life of the collective, where races have been dominated and controlled, where those who are compliant are brought into the collectives and those who are not are alienated or destroyed. Surely such an establishment, though it may have considerable influence, cannot be beneficial for its members. And yet this is the path that many in the Greater Community have taken. We do not wish to see humanity fall into such an organization. That would be a great tragedy and a loss.

◆

"How is the human perspective different from yours?"

One of the differences is that we have developed a Greater Community perspective, which is a less self-centered way of looking at the world. It is a point of view that gives great clarity and can provide great certainty regarding the smaller problems that you face in your daily affairs. If you can solve a great problem, you can solve lesser ones. You have a great problem. Every human being in the world faces this great problem. It can unite you and enable you to overcome your long-standing differences and conflicts. It is that great and that powerful. This is why we say there is a possibility for redemption within the very circumstances that threaten your well-being and your future.

> You have a great problem. Every human being in the world faces this great problem. It can unite you and enable you to overcome your long-standing differences and conflicts. It is that great and that powerful.

We know that the power of Knowledge within the individual can restore that individual and all of their relationships to a higher degree of accomplishment, recognition and ability. You must discover this for yourself.

Our lives are very different. One of the differences is that our lives are given to service, a service that we have chosen. We have the freedom to choose and thus our choice is real and meaningful and is based upon our own understanding. Amongst our group are representatives from several different worlds. We have come together in service to humanity. We represent a greater alliance that is more spiritual in nature.

◆

"This message is coming through one man. Why aren't you contacting everybody if this is so important?"

It is merely a matter of efficiency. We do not control who is selected to receive us. That is a matter for the Unseen Ones, those whom you could rightly call "Angels." We think of them in this way. They have selected this person, a person who has no position in the world, who is not recognized in the world, an individual who has been chosen because of his qualities and because of his heritage in the Greater Community. We are glad to have one through whom we can speak. If we spoke through more, they perhaps would disagree with one another, and the message would become confused and lost.

We understand, from our own studenthood, that the transmission of spiritual wisdom is generally given through one, with the support of others. This individual must bear the weight and the burden and the risk of being so chosen. We respect him for doing this, and we understand what a burden it can be. This will be misconstrued, perhaps, and that is why the wise must remain hidden. We must remain hidden. He must remain hidden. In this way, the message can be given, and the messenger can be preserved. For there will be hostility towards this message. The visitors will oppose it and are opposing it already. Their opposition can be significant but will primarily be aimed at the messenger himself. It is for this reason that the messenger must be protected.

We know that the answers to these questions will generate more questions. And many of these cannot be answered, perhaps even for a long time. The wise anywhere must live with questions that they cannot yet answer. It is through their patience and their perseverance that real answers emerge and that they are able to experience them and embody them.

Humanity is at a new beginning. It is faced with a grave situation. The need for a new education and understanding is paramount. We are here to serve this need at the request of the Unseen Ones. They are relying upon us to share our wisdom, for we live in the physical universe, as do you. We are not angelic beings. We are not perfect. We have not achieved great heights of spiritual awareness and accomplishment. And therefore our message to you about the Greater Community, we trust, will be more relevant and more easily received. The Unseen Ones know far more than we about life in the universe and about the levels of advancement and accomplishment that are available and that are practiced in many places. Yet they have asked us to speak regarding the reality of physical life because we are fully engaged there. And we have learned through our own trials and errors the importance and the meaning of what we are sharing with you.

Thus, we come as the Allies of Humanity, for such we are. Be thankful that you have allies that can help you and that can educate you and that can support your strength, your freedom and your accomplishment. For without this assistance, the prospect of your surviving the kind of alien infiltration that you are experiencing now would be very limited. Yes, there would be a few individuals who would come to realize the situation as it actually exists, but their numbers would not be great enough, and their voices would go unheard.

In this, we can only ask for your trust. We hope that through the wisdom of our words and through the opportunities you have to learn their meaning and relevance, that we can gain this trust over time, for you have allies in the Greater Community. You have great friends beyond this world who have suffered the challenges that you are facing now and have achieved success. Because we were assisted, we must now assist others. That is our sacred covenant. It is to this that we are firmly committed.

THE SOLUTION

AT ITS CORE,

THE SOLUTION TO THE INTERVENTION IS NOT ABOUT

TECHNOLOGY, POLITICS OR MILITARY FORCE.

It is about the renewal of the human spirit.

It is about people becoming aware of the Intervention

and speaking out against it.

It is about ending the isolation and the ridicule

that keep people from expressing what they see and know.

It is about overcoming fear, avoidance, fantasy and deception.

It is about people becoming strong, aware and empowered.

The Allies of Humanity provide the critical counsel that enables us
to recognize the Intervention and to offset its influences. To do this,
the Allies urge us to exercise our native intelligence and our right to
fulfill our destiny as a free race in the Greater Community.

It is time to begin.

THERE IS A NEW HOPE
IN THE WORLD

Hope in the world is rekindled by those who become strong with Knowledge. Hope can fade away and then be reignited. It can seem to come and go, depending on how people are swayed and what they choose for themselves. Hope rests with you. Because the Unseen Ones are here does not mean that there is hope, for without you, there would be no hope. For you and others like you are bringing a new hope into the world because you are learning to receive the gift of Knowledge. This brings a new hope into the world. Perhaps you cannot see this fully at this moment. Perhaps it seems beyond your understanding. But from a greater perspective, it is so very true and so very important.

The world's emergence into the Greater Community speaks to this, for if no one were preparing for the Greater Community, well, then, hope would seem to fade. And humanity's destiny would seem to be utterly predictable. But because there is hope in the world, because there is hope in you and in others like you who are responding to a greater calling, the destiny of humanity has greater promise, and the freedom of humanity may well yet be secured.

◆

FROM *STEPS TO KNOWLEDGE—CONTINUATION TRAINING*

Resistance
&
Empowerment

◆

RESISTANCE & EMPOWERMENT

The Ethics of Contact

At every turn, the Allies encourage us to take an active role in discerning and opposing the extraterrestrial Intervention that is occurring in our world today. This includes discerning our rights and priorities as the native people of this world and establishing our own Rules of Engagement concerning all present and future contact with other races of beings.

Looking at the natural world and back through human history amply demonstrates to us the lessons of intervention: that competition for resources is an integral part of nature, that intervention by one culture upon another is always carried out for self-interest and has a destructive impact on the culture and freedom of the people being discovered and that the strong always dominate the weak, if they can.

While it is conceivable that those ET races visiting our world may be an exception to this rule, such an exception would have to be proven beyond a shadow of a doubt, by giving humanity the right to assess any proposal for visitation. This has certainly not occurred. Instead, in humanity's experience of Contact so far, we have had our authority and proprietary rights as the native people of this world circumvented. The "visitors" have pursued their own agenda, without regard for humanity's approval or informed participation.

As both the Allies Briefings and much of the UFO/ET research clearly indicate, ethical contact is not occurring. While it may be appropriate for a foreign race to share with us their experience and wisdom from afar, as the Allies have done, it is not appropriate for races to come here uninvited and attempt to interfere in human affairs, even under the guise of helping us. Given the level of humanity's development at this time as a young race, it is not ethical to do this.

Humanity has not had the opportunity to establish its own Rules of Engagement or set the boundaries that every native race must establish for its own safety and security. Doing so would serve to foster human unity and cooperation because we would have to come together to accomplish this. This action would require the awareness that we are one people sharing one world, that we are not alone in the universe and that our boundaries to space must be established and protected. Tragically, this necessary developmental process is now being circumvented.

It is to encourage humanity's preparation for the realities of life in the Greater Community that the Allies Briefings were sent. Indeed, the Allies' message to humanity is a demonstration of what ethical contact really is. They are maintaining a hands-off approach, respecting our native abilities and authority while encouraging the freedom and unity that the human family is going to need in order to navigate our future in the Greater Community. While many people today doubt that humanity has the power and integrity to meet its own needs and challenges in the future, the Allies assure us that this power, the spiritual power of Knowledge, resides within all of us and that we must use it on our own behalf.

The preparation for humanity's emergence into the Greater Community has been given. The two sets of the Allies of Humanity Briefings and the books of The Greater Community Way of Knowledge are available to readers everywhere. They can be viewed at www.alliesofhumanity.org and www.newmessage.org. Together they provide the means for offsetting the Intervention and for facing our future in a changing world at the threshold of space. This is the only such preparation in the world today. It is the very preparation that the Allies have so urgently called for.

In response to the Allies Briefings, a group of dedicated readers have crafted a document entitled the Declaration of Human Sovereignty. Modeled on the United States Declaration of Independence, the Declaration of Human Sovereignty sets out to establish the Ethics of Contact and the Rules of Engagement that we, as the native people of the world, now desperately need in order to preserve human freedom and sovereignty. As the indigenous people of this world, we have the right and responsibility to determine when and how visitation will occur and who may enter our world. We must let it be known to all nations and groups in the universe who are aware of our existence that we are self-determined and intend to exercise our rights and responsibilities as an emerging race of free people in the Greater Community. The Declaration of Human Sovereignty is a beginning and can be read online at www.humansovereignty.org.

RESISTANCE & EMPOWERMENT

Taking Action – What you can do

The Allies ask us to take a stand for the well-being of our world and to become, in essence, Allies of Humanity ourselves. Yet to be real, this commitment must come from our conscience, the deepest part of ourselves. There are many things that you can do to offset the Intervention and to become a positive force by strengthening yourself and others around you.

Some readers have expressed feelings of hopelessness after reading the Allies material. If this is your experience, it is important to remember that it is the intention of the Intervention to influence you to feel either accepting and hopeful or helpless and impotent in the face of their presence. Do not allow yourself to be so persuaded. You find your strength by taking action. What can you really do? There is a great deal you can do.

◆

Educate yourself.

Preparation must begin with awareness and education. You must have an understanding of what you are dealing with. Educate yourself about the UFO/ET phenomenon. Educate yourself about the latest discoveries of planetary science and astrobiology that are becoming available to us.

RECOMMENDED READING

* See "Additional Resources" in the Appendix.

Resist the influence of the Pacification Program.

Resist the Pacification Program. Resist the influence to become listless and unresponsive to your own Knowledge. Resist the Intervention through awareness, through advocacy and through understanding. Promote human cooperation, unity and integrity.

RECOMMENDED READING

* *Greater Community Spirituality*, Chapter 6: "What is the Greater Community?" and Chapter 11: "What Is Your Preparation For?"
* *Living The Way of Knowledge*, Chapter 1: "Living in an Emerging World"

Become aware of the mental environment.

The mental environment is the environment of thought and influence in which we all live. Its effect upon our thinking, emotions and actions is even greater than the effect of the physical environment. The mental environment is now being directly affected and influenced by the Intervention. It is also being affected by government and commercial interests all around us. Becoming aware of the mental environment is crucial to maintaining your own freedom to think freely and clearly. The first step that you can take is to consciously choose who and what is influencing your thinking and decisions through the input that you receive from the outside. This includes media, books and persuasive friends, family and authority figures. Set your own guidelines and learn how to clearly determine, with discernment and objectivity, what other people, and even the culture at large, are telling you. Each of us must learn to consciously discern these influences in order to protect and uplift the mental environment in which we live.

RECOMMENDED READING

- *Wisdom from the Greater Community* Volume II, Chapter 12: "Self-expression and the Mental Environment" and Chapter 15: "Responding to the Greater Community"

◆

Study The Greater Community Way of Knowledge.

Learning The Greater Community Way of Knowledge brings you into direct contact with the deeper spiritual mind that the Creator of all life has placed within you. It is at the level of this deeper mind beyond our intellect, at the level of Knowledge, that you are safe from interference and manipulation from any worldly or Greater Community power. Knowledge also holds for you your greater spiritual purpose for coming into the world at this time. It is the very center of your spirituality. You can begin your journey in The Greater Community Way of Knowledge today by starting the study of *Steps to Knowledge* online at www.newmessage.org.

RECOMMENDED READING

- *Greater Community Spirituality,* Chapter 4: "What is Knowledge?"
- *Living The Way of Knowledge:* All chapters
- Study of *Steps to Knowledge: The Book of Inner Knowing*

◆

Form an Allies Reading Group.

To create a positive environment where the Allies material can be deeply considered, join with others to form an Allies Reading Group. We have found that when people read the Allies Briefings and the books of The Greater Community Way of Knowledge aloud with others in a supportive group setting and are free to share questions and insights as they go, their comprehension of the material grows significantly. This is one way that you can begin to find others who share your awareness and desire to know the truth about the Intervention. You can start with just one other person.

RECOMMENDED READING

- *Wisdom from the Greater Community* Volume II, Chapter 10: "Greater Community Visitations," Chapter 15: "Responding to the Greater Community," Chapter 17: "Visitors' Perceptions of Humanity," and Chapter 28: "Greater Community Realities"

- *The Allies of Humanity Book Two:* All chapters.

◆

Preserve and protect the environment.

With each passing day, we are learning more and more about the need to preserve, protect and restore our natural environment. Even if the Intervention did not exist, this would still be a priority. Yet the Allies' message gives new impetus and a new understanding for the need to create a sustainable use of our world's natural resources. Become conscious about how you live and what you consume and find what you can do to support the environment. As the Allies emphasize, our self-sufficiency as a race will be necessary to safeguard our freedom and advancement within a Greater Community of intelligent life.

RECOMMENDED READING

- *Wisdom from the Greater Community* Volume I, Chapter 14: "World Evolution"
- *Wisdom from the Greater Community* Volume II, Chapter 25: "Environments"

◆

Spread the message about
The Allies of Humanity Briefings.

Your sharing the Allies' message with others is vitally important for the following reasons:

— You help break the numbing silence that surrounds the reality and specter of the extraterrestrial Intervention.

— You help break down the isolation that keeps people from connecting with one another about this great challenge.

— You awaken those who have fallen under the influence of the Pacification Program, giving them a chance to use their own minds to re-evaluate the meaning of this phenomenon.

— You strengthen the resolve within yourself and within others not to capitulate to either fear or avoidance in meeting the great challenge of our time.

— You bring confirmation to other people's own insights and Knowledge about the Intervention.

— You help establish the resistance that can thwart the Intervention and promote the empowerment that can give humanity the unity and strength to establish our own Rules of Engagement.

HERE ARE SOME CONCRETE STEPS THAT YOU CAN TAKE TODAY:

— Share this book and its message with others. The entire first set of briefings is now available to read and to download at no cost at the Allies website: www.alliesofhumanity.org.

— Read the Declaration of Human Sovereignty and share this valuable document with others. It can be read online and printed at www.humansovereignty.org.

— Encourage your local bookstore and library to carry both volumes of *The Allies of Humanity* and the other books by Marshall Vian Summers. This increases access to the material for other readers.

— Share the Allies material and perspective in existing online forums and discussion groups whenever appropriate.

— Attend related conferences and gatherings and share the Allies' perspective.

— Translate the Allies of Humanity Briefings. If you are multilingual, please consider helping to translate the Briefings in order to make them available to more readers around the world.

— Contact New Knowledge Library to receive a free Allies advocacy packet with materials that can help you share this message with others.

RECOMMENDED READING

- *Living The Way of Knowledge,* Chapter 9: "Sharing The Way of Knowledge with Others"

- *Wisdom from The Greater Community* Volume II, Chapter 19: "Courage"

◆

This is by no means a complete list. It is merely a beginning. Look at your own life and see what opportunities may exist there, and be open to your own Knowledge and insights on this matter. In addition to doing the things listed above, people have already found creative ways to express the Allies' message—through art, through music, through poetry. Find your way.

MESSAGE FROM
MARSHALL VIAN SUMMERS

For 25 years, I have been immersed in a religious experience. This has resulted in my receiving a vast body of writings about the nature of human spirituality and humanity's destiny within a larger panorama of intelligent life in the universe. These writings, encompassed in the teaching in The Greater Community Way of Knowledge, contain a theological framework that accounts for life and the presence of God in the Greater Community, the vast expanse of space and time that we know to be our universe.

The cosmology that I have been receiving contains many messages, one of which is that humanity is emerging into a Greater Community of intelligent life and for this we must prepare. Inherent in this message is the understanding that humanity is not alone in the universe, or even alone within our own world, and that within this Greater Community, humanity will have friends, competitors and adversaries.

This larger reality was dramatically confirmed by the sudden and unexpected transmission of the first set of the Allies of Humanity Briefings in 1997. Three years earlier, in 1994, I had received the theological framework for comprehending the Allies Briefings in my book *Greater Community Spirituality: A New Revelation*. At that point, as a result of my spiritual work and writings, it became known to me that humanity has allies in the universe who are concerned about the well-being and future freedom of our race.

Within the growing cosmology that has been revealed to me is the understanding that, in the history of intelligent life in the universe, ethically advanced races have an obligation to bequeath their wisdom to young emerging races such as our own and that this bequest must take place without direct interference or intervening in the affairs of that young race. The intent here is to inform, not to interfere. This "passing down of wisdom" represents a long-existing, ethical framework regarding Contact with emerging races and how it should be conducted. The two sets of the Allies of Humanity Briefings are a clear demonstration of this model of non-interference and ethical Contact. This model should be a guiding light and a standard that we should expect other races to hold to in their attempt to contact us or to visit our world. Yet this demonstration of ethical Contact stands in stark contrast to the Intervention that is occurring in the world today.

We are moving into a position of extreme vulnerability. With the specter of resource depletion, environmental degradation and the risk of a further fracturing of the human family growing everyday, we are ripe for Intervention. We live in seeming isolation in a rich and valuable world that is being sought by others beyond our shores. We are distracted and divided and do not see the great peril intervening at our borders. It is a phenomenon that history has repeated over and over again regarding the fate of isolated native peoples who were facing intervention for the first time. We are unrealistic in our assumptions about the powers and beneficence of intelligent life in the universe. And we are only now just beginning to take stock of the condition that we have created for ourselves within our own world.

The unpopular truth is that the human family is not ready for a direct experience of Contact and certainly not ready for an intervention. We first must put our own house in order. We do not yet have the species maturity to engage with other races in the Greater Community from a position of unity, strength and discernment. And until we can reach such a position, if ever we can, then no race should attempt to directly intervene in our world. The Allies are providing us much needed wisdom and perspective, yet they are not intervening. They tell us that our fate is, and should be, in our own hands. Such is the burden of freedom in the universe.

Regardless of our lack of readiness, however, Intervention is occurring. Humanity must now prepare for this, the most consequential threshold in human history. Rather than just being casual witnesses to this phenomenon, we are at the very center of it. It is happening whether we are aware of it or not. It has the power to change the outcome for humanity. And it has everything to do with who we are and why we are here in the world at this time.

The Greater Community Way of Knowledge has been given to provide both the teaching and the preparation that we now need to face this great threshold, to renew the human spirit and to set a new course for the human family. It speaks to the urgent need for human unity and cooperation; the primacy of Knowledge, our spiritual intelligence; and the greater responsibilities we must now assume at the threshold of space. It represents a New Message from the Creator of all life.

My mission is to bring this greater cosmology and preparation into the world and with it a new hope and promise for a struggling humanity. My long preparation and the immense teaching in The Greater Community Way of Knowledge are here for this purpose. The Allies of Humanity Briefings are but a small part of this larger message. It is time now to end our ceaseless conflicts and to prepare for life in the Greater Community. To do this, we need a new understanding of ourselves as one people—the native people of this world, born of one spirituality—and of our vulnerable position as a young, emerging race in the universe. This is my message for humanity and this is why I have come.

MARSHALL VIAN SUMMERS
2008

Appendix

◆

DEFINITION OF TERMS

THE ALLIES OF HUMANITY: A small group of physical beings from the Greater Community who are hidden in the vicinity of our world in our solar system. Their mission is to observe, report and advise us on the activities of the alien visitors and intervention in the world today. They represent the wise in many worlds.

THE VISITORS: Several other alien races from the Greater Community "visiting" our world without our permission who are actively interfering in human affairs. The visitors are involved in a long process of integrating themselves into the fabric and soul of human life for the purpose of gaining control of the world's resources and people.

THE INTERVENTION: The alien visitors' presence, purpose and activities in the world.

THE PACIFICATION PROGRAM: The visitors' program of persuasion and influence aimed at disarming people's awareness and discernment of the Intervention in order to render humanity passive and compliant.

THE GREATER COMMUNITY: Space. The vast physical and spiritual universe into which humanity is emerging, which contains intelligent life in countless manifestations.

THE UNSEEN ONES: The Angels of the Creator who oversee the spiritual development of sentient beings throughout the Greater Community. The Allies refer to them as "The Unseen Ones."

HUMAN DESTINY: Humanity is destined to emerge into the Greater Community. This is our evolution.

THE COLLECTIVES: Complex hierarchical organizations composed of several alien races which are bound together by a common allegiance. There is more than one collective present in the world today to which the alien visitors belong. These collectives have competing agendas.

THE MENTAL ENVIRONMENT: The environment of thought and mental influence.

KNOWLEDGE: The spiritual intelligence that lives within each person. The Source of all that we know. Intrinsic understanding. Eternal wisdom. The timeless part of us which cannot be influenced, manipulated or corrupted. A potential in all intelligent life. Knowledge is God in you and God is all Knowledge in the universe.

THE WAYS OF INSIGHT: Various teachings in The Way of Knowledge that are taught in many worlds in the Greater Community.

THE GREATER COMMUNITY WAY OF KNOWLEDGE: A spiritual teaching from the Creator that is practiced in many places in the Greater Community. It teaches how to experience and express Knowledge and how to preserve individual freedom in the universe. This teaching has been sent here to prepare humanity for the realities of life in the Greater Community.

COMMENTS ON
THE ALLIES OF HUMANITY

I was greatly impressed with *The Allies of Humanity* . . . because the message rings true. Radar contacts, ground effects, videotape and film all prove UFOs are real. Now we must consider the real question: the agenda of their occupants. *The Allies of Humanity* forcefully confronts this issue, one which may prove critical to the future of humankind."

—JIM MARRS, author of
Alien Agenda and *Rule by Secrecy*

In light of decades spent studying both channeling and ufology/extraterrestriology, I have a very positive response to both Summers as a channel and to the message from his reported sources in this book. I am deeply impressed with his integrity as a human being, as a spirit, and as a true channel. In their message and demeanor, both Summers and his sources convincingly demonstrate to me a true service-to-other orientation in the face of so much human, and now apparently even extraterrestrial, service-to-self orientation. While serious and warning in tone, this book's message quickens my spirit with the promise of the wonders that await our species as we join the Greater Community. We must at the same time find and access our birthright relation to our Creator to ensure we are not unduly manipulated or exploited by some members of that greater community in the process."

—JON KLIMO, author of
*Channeling: Investigations on
Receiving Information from
Paranormal Sources*

Studying the UFO/Alien Abduction phenomenon for 30 years has been like piecing together a giant jigsaw puzzle. Your book, at last, gave me a framework for fitting the remaining pieces."

—ERICK SCHWARTZ,
LCSW, California

Is there a free lunch in the cosmos? *The Allies of Humanity* reminds us most forcefully, there isn't."

—ELAINE DOUGLASS,
MUFON Co-state director, Utah

The Allies will have a great echo among the Spanish-speaking population around the world. I can assure this! So many people, not only in my country, fighting for their rights to preserve their cultures! Your books only confirm what they have been trying to tell us in so many ways, for such a long time."

—INGRID CABRERA, Mexico

This book resonated deeply within me. To me, [*The Allies of Humanity*] is nothing short of groundbreaking. I honor the forces, human and otherwise, that have brought this book into being, and I pray that its urgent warning is heeded."

—RAYMOND CHONG, Singapore

Much of the Allies material resonates with what I have learned, or feel instinctively to be true."

—TIMOTHY GOOD, British UFO
researcher author of *Beyond Top
Secret* and *Unearthly Disclosure*

FURTHER STUDY

THE ALLIES OF HUMANITY addresses fundamental questions about the reality, nature and purpose of the extraterrestrial presence in the world today. However, this book raises many more questions which must be explored through further study. As such, it serves as a catalyst for greater awareness and a call to action.

To learn more, there are two tracks which the reader can follow, either separately or together. The first track is the study of the UFO/ET phenomenon itself, which has been widely documented over the last four decades by researchers representing many different points of view. In the following pages, we have listed some important resources on this subject that we feel are especially relevant to the Allies material. We encourage all readers to become more informed about this phenomenon.

The second track is for readers who would like to explore the spiritual implications of the phenomenon and what you personally can do to prepare. For this we recommend the writings of MV Summers which are listed in the following pages.

To stay informed about new materials related to the Allies of Humanity, please visit the Allies website at: www.alliesofhumanity. org. For more information about The Greater Community Way of Knowledge, please visit: www.newmessage.org.

ADDITIONAL RESOURCES

Below is a preliminary list of resources on the subject of the UFO/ ET phenomenon. It is not intended by any means to be an exhaustive bibliography on the subject, merely a place to start. Once your research into the reality of the phenomenon has begun, there will be more and more materials for you to explore, both by these and other sources. Discernment is always advised.

BOOKS

Berliner, Don: *UFO Briefing Document*, Dell Publishing, 1995.

Bryan, C.D.B.: *Close Encounters of the Fourth Kind: Alien Abduction, UFOs and the Conference at MIT*, Penguin, 1996.

Dolan, Richard: *UFOs and the National Security State: Chronology of a Coverup, 1941-1973*, Hampton Roads Publishing, 2002.

Fowler, Raymond E.: *The Allagash Abductions: Undeniable Evidence of Alien Intervention*, 2nd Edition, Granite Publishing, LLC, 2005.

Good, Timothy: *Unearthly Disclosure*, Arrow Books, 2001.

Grinspoon, David: *Lonely Planets: The Natural Philosophy of Alien Life*, Harper Collins Publishers, 2003.

Hopkins, Budd: *Missing Time*, Ballantine Books, 1988.

Howe, Linda Moulton: *An Alien Harvest,* LMH Productions, 1989.

Jacobs, David: *The Threat: What the Aliens Really Want,* Simon & Schuster, 1998.

Mack, John E.: *Abduction: Human Encounters with Aliens,* Charles Scribner's Sons, 1994.

Marrs, Jim: *Alien Agenda: Investigating the Extraterrestrial Presence Among Us,* Harper Collins, 1997.

Sauder, Richard: *Underwater and Underground Bases,* Adventures Unlimited Press, 2001.

Turner, Karla: *Taken: Inside the Alien-Human Abduction Agenda,* Berkeley Books, 1992.

DVDs

The Alien Agenda and the Ethics of Contact with Marshall Vian Summers, MUFON Symposium, 2006. Available through New Knowledge Library.

The ET Intervention and Control in the Mental Environment, with Marshall Vian Summers, Conspiracy Con, 2007. Available through New Knowledge Library.

Out of the Blue: The Definitive Investigation of the UFO Phenomenon, Hanover House, 2007. To order: http://outofthebluethe-movie.com/

WEBSITES

www.humansovereignty.org

www.alliesofhumanity.org

www.newmessage.org

THE GREATER COMMUNITY
WAY OF KNOWLEDGE

THE WRITINGS OF
MV SUMMERS

GREATER COMMUNITY SPIRITUALITY: A New Revelation. Provides new answers to 27 fundamental questions about the meaning of life, our relationship with God and our destiny, all from a Greater Community perspective. The "Theology of Contact" for understanding the reality and the spirituality of intelligent life in the universe.

ISBN 978-1-884238-21-5: 27 chapters, 384 pages: Trade Paper: $17.95

STEPS TO KNOWLEDGE: The Book of Inner Knowing. A profound guide to experiencing and applying Knowledge, the greater Spiritual Intelligence that lives within you. The preparation book for humanity's emergence into a Greater Community of intelligent life. The Book of Practice in The Greater Community Way of Knowledge. Winner of the "Year 2000 Book of the Year Award" for Spirituality.

ISBN 978-1-884238-18-5: 365 practices,
520 pages: Trade Paper: $19.95

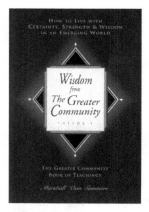

WISDOM FROM THE GREATER COMMU-NITY, Volume I: How to Live with Certainty, Strength and Wisdom in an Emerging World. The Greater Community Teaching on topics ranging from "Marriage" and "Achieving Peace" to "Provoking Change" and "World Evolution." 35 Chapters. The First Book of Discourses in The Greater Community Way of Knowledge.

ISBN 978-1-884238-11-6: 35 chapters,
448 pages: Trade Paper: $25.

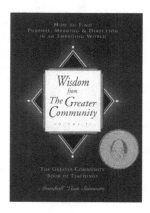

WISDOM FROM THE GREATER COM-MUNITY, Volume II: How to Find Purpose, Meaning and Direction in an Emerging World. The Greater Community Teaching on topics ranging from "Discernment" and "Solving Problems" to "Environments" and "Visitors' Perceptions of Humanity." 34 Chapters. The Second Book of Discourses in The Greater Community Way of Knowledge. Silver Award Finalist in the 1997 Benjamin Franklin Book Award for Spirituality.

ISBN 978-1-884238-12-3: 34 chapters,
448 pages: Trade Paper: $25.

LIVING THE WAY OF KNOWLEDGE: Building the Foundation for Becoming a Man or Woman of Knowledge in an Emerging World. How to bring the grace, the guidance and the power of Knowledge into the "Four Pillars" of your life: your relationships, your work, your health and your spiritual direction. After *Steps to Knowledge*, the second great practice for learning and living The Way of Knowledge.

ISBN 978-1-884238-03-1: 11 chapters,
168 Pages: Wire Bound: $20.
Currently available only through New Knowledge Library.

RELATIONSHIPS & HIGHER PURPOSE: Finding Your People, Your Purpose and Your Mission in the World. A lifelong resource for discovering and fulfilling your true purpose for coming into the world. Reveals the source of each person's deep yearning for true relationship and offers a revolutionary understanding of those key relationships that will change your life. Not merely a book to read, but a companion book meant to be studied, deeply considered and applied.

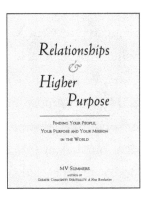

ISBN 978-1-884238-87-1: 15 chapters.
192 Pages: Wire Bound: $30
Currently available only through New Knowledge Library.

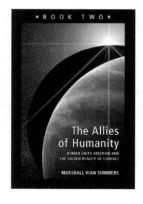

ALLIES OF HUMANITY, BOOK TWO: Human Unity, Freedom and the Hidden Reality of Contact. Continues the Allies' vital message to humanity begun in Book One. Provides new information about the interaction between races in our local universe and about the most dangerous aspects of the Intervention as it advances its hidden agenda in the world. A must-read for anyone who is concerned about the future and freedom of humanity.

ISBN 978-1-884238-35-2: 6 Briefings and 3 Commentaries, 205 pages: Trade paper, $14.95.

The Books of The Greater Community Way of Knowledge can be requested at your local bookstore or ordered from an online bookseller. You can also order directly from us at New Knowledge Library. At this time *Living The Way of Knowledge* and *Relationships & Higher Purpose* can be ordered only from New Knowledge Library at nkl@greatercommunity.org or (303) 938-8401. For book orders outside of Colorado please call 1-800-938-3891. To view the Books of Knowledge in greater detail, please visit our website at www.newknowledgelibrary.org.

Note: All books are available at www.newknowledgelibrary.org in print or ebook format.

EXCERPTS FROM THE BOOKS OF THE GREATER COMMUNITY WAY OF KNOWLEDGE

"You are not merely a human being in this one world. You are a citizen of the Greater Community of worlds. This is the physical universe that you recognize through your senses. It is far greater than you can now comprehend... You are a citizen of a greater physical universe. This acknowledges not only your Lineage and your Heritage but also your purpose in life at this time, for the world of humanity is growing into the life of the Greater Community of worlds. This is known to you, though your beliefs may not yet account for it."

> —*Steps to Knowledge:*
> Step 187: I am a citizen of the
> Greater Community of Worlds

"You have come into the world at a great turning point, a turning point only part of which you will see in your own lifetime. It is a turning point where your world gains contact with the worlds in its vicinity. This is the natural evolution of humanity, as it is the natural evolution of all intelligent life in all worlds."

> —*Steps to Knowledge:*
> Step 190: The world is
> emerging into the Greater
> Community of worlds and that
> is why I have come

"You have great friends beyond this world. That is why humanity is seeking to enter into the Greater Community because the Greater Community represents a broader range of its true relationships. You have true friends beyond the world because you are not alone in the world and you are not alone in the Greater Community of worlds. You have friends beyond this world because your Spiritual Family has its representatives everywhere. You have friends beyond this world because you are working not merely on the evolution of your world but on the evolution of the universe as well. Beyond your imagination, beyond your conceptual capabilities, this is most certainly true."

> —*Steps to Knowledge:*
> Step 211: I have great friends
> beyond this world.

"Do not react with hope. Do not react with fear. Respond with Knowledge."

> —*Wisdom from the Greater*
> *Community Volume II*
> Chapter 10: Greater Community
> Visitations

"Why is this happening?" Science cannot answer that. Reason cannot answer that. Wishful thinking cannot answer that. Fearful self-protection cannot answer that. What can answer that? You must ask this question with a different kind of mind, see with different kinds of eyes and have a different experience here."

—Wisdom from the Greater
Community Volume II
Chapter 10: Greater Community
Visitations

"You must think of God now in the Greater Community—not a human God, not a God of your written history, not a God of your trials and tribulations, but a God for all time, for all races, for all dimensions, for those who are primitive and for those who are advanced, for those who think like you and for those who think so differently, for those who believe and for those for whom belief is inexplicable. This is God in the Greater Community. And this is where you must begin."

—Greater Community Spirituality
Chapter 1: What is God?

"You are needed in the world. It is time to prepare. It is time to become focused and determined. There is no escape from this, for only those who are developed in The Way of Knowledge will have capability in the future and will be able to maintain their freedom in a mental environment that will be increasingly influenced by the

Greater Community."

> —*Living The Way of Knowledge:*
> Chapter 6: The Pillar of
> Spiritual Development

"There are no heroes here. There is no one to worship. There is a foundation to be built. There is work to be done. There is a preparation to undergo. And there is a world to serve."

> —*Living The Way of Knowledge:*
> Chapter 6: The Pillar of
> Spiritual Development

"The Greater Community Way of Knowledge is being presented into the world, where it is unknown. It has no history and no background here. People are not used to it. It does not necessarily fit in with their ideas, beliefs or expectations. It does not conform to the world's current religious understanding. It comes in a naked form—without ritual and pageantry, without wealth and excess. It comes purely and simply. It is like a child in the world. It is seemingly vulnerable, and yet it represents a Greater Reality and a greater promise for humanity."

> —*Sacred Writings:*
> unpublished

"There are those in the Greater Community who are more powerful than you. They can outsmart you, but only if you are not looking.

They can affect your mind, but they cannot control it if you are with Knowledge."

—Living The Way of Knowledge:
Chapter 10: Being Present
in the World

"Humanity lives in a very big house. Part of the house is on fire. And others are visiting here to determine how the fire can be put out for their benefit."

—Living The Way of Knowledge:
Chapter 11: Preparing for the
Future

"Go out on a clear night and look up. Your destiny is there. Your difficulties are there. Your opportunities are there. Your redemption is there."

—Greater Community Spirituality:
Chapter 15: Who Serves
Humanity?

"You should never assume that there is a greater logic in an advanced race, unless it is strong with Knowledge. In fact, they may be as fortified against Knowledge as you are. Old habits, rituals, structures and authorities must be challenged by the evidence of Knowledge. That is why even in the Greater Community, the man or woman of Knowledge is a powerful force."

—Steps to Knowledge:
Upper Levels

"Your fearlessness in the future must not be born of pretense, but born of your certainty in Knowledge. In this way, you will be a refuge of peace and a source of wealth for others. This is what you are meant to be. This is why you have come into the world."

—*Steps to Knowledge:*
Step 162: I will not be afraid today.

"It is not an easy time to be in the world, but if contribution is your purpose and intention, it is the right time to be in the world."

—*Greater Community Spirituality:*
Chapter 11: What Is Your
Preparation for?

"In order for you to carry out your mission, you must have great allies because God knows you cannot do it alone."

—*Greater Community Spirituality:*
Chapter 12: Whom Will You Meet?

"The Creator would not leave humanity without a preparation for the Greater Community. And for this, The Greater Community Way of Knowledge is being presented. It is born of the Great Will of the universe. It is communicated through the Angels of the universe who serve the emergence of Knowledge everywhere and who cultivate relationships that can embody Knowledge everywhere. This work is the work of the Divine in the world, not to bring you to the Divine, but to bring you to the world, for the world needs you. That is why you were sent here. That is why you have chosen to come. And you have chosen to come to serve and support the world's emergence into the Greater Community, for that is the great need of humanity at this time, and that great need will overshadow all of the needs of humanity in the times to come."

—*Greater Community Spirituality:*
Introduction

ABOUT THE AUTHOR

Though he is little known in the world today, Marshall Vian Summers may ultimately be recognized as the most significant spiritual teacher to emerge in our lifetime. For more than twenty years he has been quietly writing and teaching a spirituality that acknowledges the undeniable reality that humanity lives in a vast and populated universe and now urgently needs to prepare for its emergence into a Greater Community of intelligent life.

MV Summers teaches the discipline of *Knowledge*, or inner knowing. "Our deepest intuition," he says, "is but an external expression of the great power of Knowledge." His books *Steps to Knowledge: The Book of Inner Knowing,* winner of the Year 2000 Book of the Year Award for Spirituality in the United States, and *Greater Community Spirituality: A New Revelation* together comprise a foundation that could be considered the first "Theology of Contact." The entire body of his work, some twenty volumes, only a handful yet currently published by New Knowledge Library, may well represent some of the most original and advanced spiritual teachings to appear in modern history. He is also the founder of The Society for The Greater Community Way of Knowledge, a religious non-profit organization.

With *The Allies of Humanity,* Marshall Vian Summers becomes perhaps the first major spiritual teacher to sound a clear warning about the true nature of the Intervention now occurring in the world, calling for personal responsibility, preparation, and collective aware-ness. He has devoted his life to receiving The Greater Community Way of Knowledge, a gift to humanity from the Creator. He is com-mitted to bringing this New Message from God into the world. To read about the New Message online, please visit www.newmessage.org.

ABOUT THE SOCIETY

The Society for The Greater Community Way of Knowledge has a great mission in the world. The Allies of Humanity have presented the problem of the Intervention and all that it portends. In response to this grave challenge, a solution has been given in the spiritual teaching called The Greater Community Way of Knowledge. This teaching provides the Greater Community perspective and spiritual preparation that humanity will need in order to maintain our right of self-determination and to successfully take our place as an emerging world within a larger universe of intelligent life.

The mission of The Society is to present this New Message for humanity through its publications, internet websites, educational programs and contemplative services and retreats. The Society's goal is to develop men and women of Knowledge who will be the first to pioneer a Greater Community preparation in the world today and to begin to offset the impact of the Intervention. These men and women will be responsible for keeping Knowledge and wisdom alive in the world as the struggle for humanity's freedom intensifies.

The Society was founded in 1992 as a religious non-profit organization by Marshall Vian Summers. Over the years, a group of dedicated students has been gathering to directly assist him. The Society has been supported and maintained by this core of devoted students who are committed to bringing a new spiritual awareness and preparation into the world. The Society's mission requires the support and participation of many more people. Given the gravity of the world's condition, there is an urgent need for Knowledge and preparation. Thus, The Society is calling men and women everywhere to assist us in giving the gift of this New Message to the world at this critical turning point in our history.

As a religious non-profit organization, The Society has been supported entirely through voluntary activity, tithes and contributions. However, the growing need to reach and prepare people around the world is surpassing The Society's ability to fulfill its mission.

You can become a part of this great mission through your contribution. Share the Allies' message with others. Help raise the awareness of the fact that we are one people and one world emerging into a greater arena of intelligent life. Become a student of The Way of Knowledge. And if you are in a position to be a benefactor for this great undertaking or if you know someone who is, please contact The Society. Your contribution is needed now in order to make possible the dissemination of the Allies' critical message worldwide and to help turn the tide for humanity.

◆

"You stand at the threshold of receiving
something of the greatest magnitude,
something that is needed in the world—
something that is being transferred
to the world and translated into
the world.

You are among the first
who will receive this.

Receive it well."

GREATER COMMUNITY SPIRITUALITY

THE SOCIETY FOR THE GREATER COMMUNITY
WAY OF KNOWLEDGE

P.O. Box 1724 • Boulder, CO 80306-1724
(303) 938-8401, fax (303) 938-1214
society@greatercommunity.org
www.alliesofhumanity.org   www.newmessage.org